Other Books by Jane Lí Fox

The Pocketbook of Prosperity, Peace and Personal Power
The Pocketbook of Relationships
The Pocketbook of Transformation and Transcendence
(the above were co-authored with Karen Cornell and Marleen Putnam)

Feng Shui for Horses

When God Wears Fur

by Jane Lí Fox

FIRST EDITION
First Printing, 2010

Fox, Jane Lí—
        When God Wears Fur /
Jane Lí Fox—1ˢᵗ ed.

        c.   cm.
        ISBN: 978-0-9830590-0-4

Bronze Horse Publications does not have any authority concerning private business transactions between our authors and the public. If you wish to contact the author or would like more information about this book, please write to the author in care of Bronze Horse Publications and we will forward your request. Please write to:

Jane Lí Fox
Bronze Horse Publications
janelifox@yahoo.com

Introduction

No doubt, many of you reading this book are aware that "God" spelled backwards is "Dog." Nothing could be more apropos. Dogs for the most part are the epitome of unconditional love. We humans do not have to do a darn thing to acquire the unconditional love of a dog.

I have asked myself the question many times over, "What causes us to remember some things and forget others?" The answer is simple: "attachment." The things we let go of completely we are more apt to forget. After all, it stands to reason, doesn't it? This is primarily why I am writing this book.

I am choosing to remember some profound events that have affected me in a way that, really and truly, cannot be expressed entirely. The "limitless" cannot be described by limiting words, and yet at the same time I believe words can move us to a point where we can make a shift within ourselves to open up in a way that resembles a door opening to dimensions we never thought possible.

This book is about the life of our beloved dog, Phoenix. He departed this world November 8, 2006. However, I believe Phoenix represents all dogs, all breeds, the world over. He was for me, and my family, God wearing fur.

Jane Li

Dedication

This book is dedicated to our beloved
and most precious dog, Phoenix.
His unwavering loyalty and "presence" helped me
to awaken on so many levels
by being an example day after day of love
without condition for almost sixteen years.

Thank you, dear Phoenix, for being willing
to be a door of expansion for all.

You will always be remembered.

Magic with Miracles

I live in the world of the miraculous.

In this world
there is no want, no poverty, no war, no illness.

It is the world where hummingbirds abound,
horses dance,
dogs take people for walks,
and the sun never rises because the sun never sets.

In this world there is only joy
and the sound of laughter that is echoed everywhere.

The trees give hugs,
squirrels bring people food,
and crows weave magic with their wings.

There are rainbows at every turn,
spiders that talk,
and children are the teachers.

This is the world of love without end,
born of love, so it continues in love.

It is a world free of judgment
so all can be who they are
in endless perfection, infinite joy,
and infinite abundance.

This world does indeed exist,
and it is not just unique to me.

It exists for each and every one of us
when our hearts become willing to see.

Jane Li

Note to the Reader

This is a book of transformation. It is a door that has the potential for awakening us all by way of the magic and the miracles that we begin to notice when we simply become willing to open that door.

Even though the first chapter may be a bit challenging for those who have lost their beloved dogs, please continue reading. You may be guided to begin to view all of life in a new and magical way.

I would encourage all who pick up this book to open your heart, let go, and allow love without condition to begin its transformation and become part of your reality…

…forever.

Jane Li

Acknowledgments

I am deeply grateful to everyone, including my family, who inspired the contents of this book and its 'coming together' in a most profound and unique fashion. I would also like to thank all of the following people with the utmost appreciation and love:

Thank you, David Fox (my former husband), whose friendship, love, and support continue to encourage me and my endeavors.

Thank you, Dr. Richard Bartlett, DC, ND who, through his books and Matrix Energetics seminars (www.matrixenergetics.com), helped me to expand light years beyond what I ever dreamed possible.

Thank you, Beverly McCaw, for having spent countless hours accurately typing and editing my handwritten manuscripts, and still being a stellar friend to me.

Thank you, to my dear friend Kaya, who has been a timely mirror for me and helped inspire the title for this book.

Thank you, CeCe Fultz for your unwavering support of me as a writer.

Thank you, Kathy Oman (designer of this cover and outstanding creative photographer – www.kathyoman.com) for having used your intuition to capture the essence of this book.

Many thanks with love also, for all of my clients and their beloved dogs that provided me with pictures for this book. Dog picture providers include:

> Doug and Suzanne Eichner with children, Nate and Cade: the loving "family" of Spencer
> Susanne Sherburne, loving "mother" of Sasha
> Joe and Pat Callihan; proud "parents" of Cassie
> Gayle Hayward; loving "mother" of Gruffud
> Jerry and Paula; loving "family" for Tuck, also referred to as "the Tuckster"
> Skip and Sun Lí Thompson; proud "parents" of Spanky Lí
> James Ross, for allowing his dear V-Dog to appear in this book
> Eleanor and Neal Blacker, for sharing Wally with us

Also, I wish to give a special "Thank You" to Lleyn Moss, whose honor and love for the animals is a true inspiration.

Table of Contents

1

Remembrance
(In Transition)

It was a glorious sunny day in the crisp and gorgeously green Pacific Northwest. A perfect day one might say, and after numerous days of relentless rain, we were all more than ready for the sun's surprising appearance. It was a day to remember, as well as a day to forget. In the words of the Hopi Indian Tribe, "It was a good day to die."

As Phoenix was readying himself for his next "adventure," I was busy contemplating this event we all call "death." For many years now, I have chosen to call it "transition." It just seems softer somehow. Yet we just are never quite prepared when it comes. Even after a long illness, one would think it would be easier to accept. But really, what is easy about never seeing our loved ones in the way we have always known them in a physical form? We miss the contact, the smiles, the words, "I love you," the breath, and the smells.

What I have found to be most interesting is that I have had people tell me they missed their dog more when they died, than they missed their spouse at their passing. For me, I have no judgment about those people because I understand why they feel the way they do. The dog loved them without condition; sometimes we as spouses do not. Dogs have no hidden "agendas," so when it comes time for the transition all that's left behind is peace; at least on the part of the dog. For us two-legged species it can feel like a huge void for a very long time.

I quickly returned from my mental meanderings. Now, right now, was all that mattered and I wanted to greet it with love and courage for the upcoming task, because the time had come. My son Jesse and I were in our veterinarian's office with our dear dog Phoenix for the very last time.

The night before, I had driven over to my former husband's apartment to see Phoenix after an urgent phone call from David. Phoenix was almost sixteen years old, which is pretty aged for a Sheltie. At the time we purchased him, the breeder told us the average life span for this particular breed was fourteen years. No doubt, we have been "blessed" to have him so long.

About one and one half years earlier, when our thirty-two year marriage ended, Phoenix lived with me. He had slowed down quite considerably; but was still able to walk up the two short steps outside our home. However, within about six months we had to move to an apartment with many more stairs. Precious Phoenix just could not make this grade. I was happy to carry him up and down the stairs, but over time I realized it had become overly taxing for me. Phoenix weighed about forty pounds as he was "oversized" for his breed. I knew I had to choose what would be the best for everyone involved, including myself, and at that time, decided to ask David if Phoenix could come live with him.

Knowing I would have to part with my beloved Phoenix then was extremely difficult as my precious dog and I had been inseparable for fourteen years. So still with much reservation, I made the call to David. He lived in a third floor apartment with many more stairs, but David was a whole lot stronger and larger than I was. Without a glitch in his voice David's words rolled out like water off a duck's back, "Of course I'll take care of him." A sense of relief washed over me followed by fear. For the first time in over thirty-five years, I would be completely alone. (At the time, I had no idea what a gift this would turn out to be. After spending most of my life in the daily chaos of "survival," I was now on my way to making peace with my self by finding myself in a pile of self-created ashes. What seemed like the absolute worst time of my life was also the time that a spark ignited in my soul.)

Honestly, in some odd way I was comforted then that Phoenix would now be with David. It was a connecting point between us. David's health had been so unstable for so long and I had great concern for him. You just do not live with someone for thirty-two years and not care anymore (at least for me). But what was most curious to me was that I began to see a magnificent tapestry that was being woven by unseen hands, and saw just how these furry creatures we call dogs can transform our "reality" or what we call "reality" into a vast array of magical experiences, if we have the heart to see.

I gathered Phoenix's belongings, which consisted of a basket of toys, a blanket, and his leash, and drove him to David's apartment. The following months I visited Phoenix frequently and took him out for very short walks around the complex. He just could not walk very far. His legs and feet could barely carry him. I would tell him as we walked, that soon he would get to trade in his old tired body for a new one.

Then, last night, after an urgent call from David regarding Phoenix's rapidly deteriorating condition, I drove immediately to his apartment. I knew in my heart it was coming time for dear Phoenix to be on his way and that he might not make it through the night. I flew up the stairs as if I had sprouted wings and then knocked. The door opened slowly, revealing David in tears. He not only was exhausted but clearly distraught as well. His words were few. He pointed to the living room. As I walked ever so quietly, I was astounded to see the entire floor covered with painting tarps. Within seconds, I knew why. There were bloodstains everywhere. Phoenix was hemorrhaging internally and yet there he was lying so peaceful and calm in the corner. I was silently wishing he would just go to sleep that night and not awaken. I felt it would be so much easier. I thought of a saying I once heard that went, "If you want to make God laugh, tell Him your plans." So often, we think we know what would be best. What I have come to accept is that it doesn't matter what we think we know, but what matters is our capacity to love.

I placed a call to our youngest son Jesse. He lived close by and I wanted to afford him the opportunity to say his "goodbyes" in the event that Phoenix did not awaken the following morning. Jesse came immediately. By this time, David had disappeared into his bedroom and Jesse and I took turns gently stroking Phoenix. I could see in my mind's eye that it would be the two of us taking Phoenix to the vet in the morning had he not passed on his own. It is most important to honor our feelings as well as others', especially during these tender and vulnerable times. Some people just cannot be present when their animals are "put to sleep," and others would not miss it for the world.

About a year and a half prior to this event, I had to have my beloved horse, Prince, put to sleep. After everyone had gone that afternoon, I sat with him in his pasture for two hours after he had departed. It was one of the most moving and honoring experiences of my entire life. Yet, I did not want to be there the next day when his body was taken away. At that time, David and I were still together and he said he would go instead. So, we all have our parts to play on different stages at different times, and our roles change as well … sometimes quite abruptly.

In preparation for this time of Phoenix's passing, I made a special blanket for him, which I still possess as a keepsake. I called it his "Transition" blanket. The blanket, of a beautiful royal blue with gold fleece, is wrapped around the body of the animal when used. On it, framed within a circle, it bears meaningful symbols which represent "heaven" and "transition." Around the perimeter of the circle is the message, "Thank you, Phoenix, for all the unconditional love." For me this event of transition is sacred. It is similar to the event of birth because we are only there once for both. Be it humans or animals, the tendency is to speak quietly and walk softly so as not to disturb the sacred process. I liken it to falling snow; caressing the earth with a magical white blanket, it speaks of silence without the utterance of words; and at the heart level, we "get it." We "get" that the most meaningful and wondrous events are "birthed" in this silence. These are the times that contain the potential to change our lives forever because the answers we are so desperately searching for are hidden amidst the silence.

In my view, dogs seem to depart this world with dignity and an acceptance of knowing they did their very best. They had fulfilled their mission with "No regrets."

At David's apartment that last night, Phoenix was resting so peacefully that I decided it was time for me to return home for some rest myself. I told Jesse he should probably do the same. We agreed to see what the next day would bring and he said he would be there to help in any way he could. We each said good night to Phoenix and headed for home. I left with great hesitancy. I so much wanted to bring Phoenix home with me and have him sleep next to me one last time, but it was not to be. He needed to be exactly where he was, but what I did return home with were precious memories. I reminisced about all of the many times he had been my shadow. Whether I was sick, injured, or just plain tired, Phoenix was always there and that was his most favorite place to be, next to me. At times, it felt to me as if he had come into this world just to be my personal guardian. Of course, he loved our entire family, but it was clear Phoenix was "my" dog.

I found myself basking in the "essence" of the unconditional love he had for me, and at the same time, painfully aware that the end of an era had come. Phoenix was the "link' that kept David and me in contact. Outside of this dynamic, there was not much else to talk about. My heart sank in my chest as if a five hundred pound anchor had just been tied to it. As much as we wish it to be otherwise, nothing remains the same, but what I have come to know and love is that the magical side of life is found in the unknown.

The next thing I knew it was morning, and as I slowly awakened, I felt as if a veil was being removed from my being. Even though I felt as if I could and wanted to sleep forever, I had remarkable clarity. The first question I posed to the universe at large was, "Is Phoenix still with us?" The answer was swooped to me as if being delivered by carrier pigeon, and it came very direct and succinct. "Yes!" Oh, I thought, now it really felt bittersweet. Just the night before I had wished he would not have awakened, and now I felt a sense of joy that I could still see him alive again one last time. But, more than that, he would see me. He would know that dear Jesse and I were going to help him to be on his way.

When God Wears Fur

I was feeling a myriad of emotions that spanned anywhere from joy to an overwhelming sense of grief. I knew one thing was for certain, and that was in a few short hours Jesse and I would be at our vet's office saying good-bye to our beloved Phoenix. But the much larger reality was that I would be saying good-bye to what I knew to be one of the best friends I had ever had ... no exceptions. So, after downing massive amounts of caffeine I made my way once again to David's apartment. I had phoned Jesse and we agreed to meet there at nine a.m.

As I drove to David's, I began to feel such a profound feeling of gratitude for our son Jesse. Until recently, for many years, our relationship was extremely strained — and that was an understatement. Years before David and I separated, our home life for the most part was constant chaos. Unspoken anger hung above our dwelling like tinsel on a Christmas tree. None of us had much to say to the other. Little did I know that beneath all of this so-called chaos, a bond was being created between the three of us — David, Jesse, and myself — that would not be visible for quite some time. The enormity of what our dog had been tirelessly trying to show us was about to be birthed. It was as if Phoenix himself had created a play and we were all learning our parts and now it was "Showtime."

When I arrived at David's, it seemed like I had been transported there in "nanoseconds." Everything seemed so "surreal," as I made my way, once again, to the third floor. Jesse was already inside with Phoenix, and David, overcome with grief, had already secluded himself. Phoenix was very alert and calm, waiting for us to assist him. Jesse and I wrapped him in his "Transition" blanket ever so gingerly and quietly. Then Jesse gathered him up in his arms as a father would gather his newborn, and out we went.

My mind wandered and focused upon the many times I had carried him up and down the stairs, and truly, I was honored to do it. And, why wouldn't I be? This precious little being ("God" disguised in fur) had absorbed *energetically* many "wounds" of the dysfunctional people he had lived with, myself included.

My thought was then carried back to the present moment. Yes, this would be the last time he was carried down the stairs. When we got to the car, I opened the back door of Jesse's red Ford Focus. Jesse very delicately and precisely placed Phoenix on the seat, and quietly closed the door. We began our sacred journey. I knew Phoenix felt comforted by Jesse's presence. And, as for me, well, I was so grateful I did not have to do this alone. After what appeared to be so much loss the past two years, sometimes the presence of a loved one can mean so much.

I would describe Jesse as a noble spirit of quiet acquiescence coupled with exuberant power all rolled into one thin tall body. One of the things I love and appreciate about him is his ability to be silent. For most people silence can be difficult. I believe when we are at home in our own skin, silence is not a problem. In the last two years, Jesse and I were more often than not, on the "same page." We also at times knew what the other was thinking. We both knew that particular day that our beloved Phoenix had been a catalyst for our entire family, a catalyst of joy. It is what dogs are all about, really. Think about it. When we arrive home at the end of the day, who is usually the one most excited to see us? Without question, it is the dog! Dogs don't lie around all day thinking about our faults and shortcomings and all of the things that need to be "discussed' when we get home. They are always in the present moment, and that spells joy.

As Jesse drove, I was busy projecting about what was about to come. Time seemed to stand still as if we had entered a parallel "reality" in which everything seemed surreal ... "Mom, is this where I turn?" This question broke the silence and I was suddenly "snapped back' into the "current' reality, where I softly replied, "Yes." It was then I returned to a reality of deep contemplation regarding the polarity of beginnings and endings. In that place I asked myself this question, "Is there anything that matters?" The answer came swiftly; "Relationships." All of life is embodied in that one word. What I have come to realize and embrace is that the most important relationship we will ever have, bar none, is with ourselves. But, we are always relating to something be it other people, our animal friends, plants, or other forms of life. Unfortunately, good portions of these relationships end in disappointment because we had "agendas." We wanted something. We just were not relating for the sheer joy of it.

Dogs, however, are in a category all their own. Have you ever noticed for example that a dog will bring its toy or ball to anyone who could potentially be a player? And, have you also noticed; they do not give up, and are usually persistent until they find someone to play? What a testimony this is for humans. More often than not, we end up sulking in the corner and even at times have a major "meltdown" if we hear the word, "No." We think there is something horribly wrong with us if someone we choose to play with does not respond, or if they do, it is not what we expected. We fail to realize that the entire universe is our playground and the playmates are inexhaustible. We've only begun to assimilate the love and lessons to be learned from these precious bundles of fur and fun.

When God Wears Fur

We pulled into the parking lot of the veterinarian's clinic. As the car engine was silenced, we sat for a few moments. Back in a time capsule I went. Two years prior I had taken Phoenix in for quite a "serious' operation. I had a two and a half pound tumor removed from his side. We just did not know how it was going to go. But shortly afterward, it was evident the surgery had given him a new lease on life. He made a miraculous recovery at the age of thirteen, as this was not common. However, this time it was very different. I knew he would not be coming home with us ever again, at least not in the form of a dog, but rather in the form of ash.

Slowly Jesse emerged from the car and opened the rear door. He removed Phoenix from the back seat as one would remove a rare artifact from an archeological dig. We made our way to the entrance, and I opened the door for Jesse and Phoenix. We were solemnly greeted, and directed to exam room number two. Phoenix was well known, and loved by all of the staff there, who were very familiar with his current health struggles. This dreaded day that we all knew was inevitable and immanent, was now here. The three of us entered the exam room. Jesse placed Phoenix on the exam table. What seemed like eternity was only about seven minutes, when finally the kind East Indian man entered the room. He looked at Phoenix, and then his eyes moved to meet Jesse's, then mine. He then asked very quietly, "Is it time?" I took a deep breath and said, "Yes."

I often marvel at the weight that one simple "yes" can carry. The doctor left the room to prepare for the injection. Jesse and I kept stroking Phoenix and reassuring him of just how much we loved him and that soon his physical struggle would be over. But truth be told it was really Phoenix that was reassuring us that he was not going anywhere. I've come to realize that what we call death is merely a transition; a change of form. It is nothing to fear, but the tendency is to be afraid of the unknown, or things we think we have not yet experienced. One thing was for sure, and that was the unexplained sense of true calm that was presiding over the exam room that day. It felt as if we were all in a state of suspended animation cocooned inside a warm blanket of love and care, like Phoenix was in his "Transition" blanket. As the doctor entered for the second time I knew all of us were as ready as we ever were going to be. I pulled my chair over to the exam table so that I was sitting directly below Phoenix's head. I wanted us to be eye to eye until his very last breath. I wanted to be the last thing Phoenix saw. I wanted him to know that I was with him and loved him until the very end of his physical lifetime.

The injection was administered. After a few moments lapsed, I began to see what appeared to be a fine white vapor emerging from Phoenix's eyes. It was exiting as a mist, which began forming circles. The circles then appeared to be getting larger and higher. It felt to me as if a joyous dance was occurring right before me. I blinked and it was gone. I have heard the eyes are the "windows" to the soul. I don't know about that, but what I do know is that Phoenix was so glad to be rid of his old tired body. Still as glad as I was that he was free, I was painfully aware that his passing would leave an enormous void, because his loving presence had been so expansive.

Jesse and I lingered for a time. We stroked his body in honor and silence for what this dear little dog had brought to our lives for so many years. There was absolutely no question in my mind that day. I knew God had truly visited us in a fur coat; one that I would carry in my heart, forever. It's curious how at times like this, we just intuitively know when its time to go. As Jesse and I left the room that day, I turned to Phoenix and spoke what I believe are two of the most powerful words we can ever say, and they were the only two words that seemed fitting: "Thank you."

Gruffud

2

Homecoming

"There is no greater homecoming than coming home to oneself."
- Jane Li

Sixteen years ago, one quiet, beautiful summer morning in early August, I said to my husband, David, "I want to look at dogs today." The sky was an exotic shade of blue, almost crystalline. There was a magical quality to it. David responded, "Well, Jane Lí, do you have any idea to where we could go do that?" He went on to say, "I don't know of any pet stores that have puppies, do you?" I replied, "No, but perhaps we can go to the animal shelter, I've heard that there has been many a fabulous find at those places." So off we went. I was beyond excitement! "Exhilarated" was a more accurate term to describe how I felt inside. I had wanted a dog for as long as I could remember.

Up to that point in our almost twenty-year marriage, a dog was never part of the equation. The homes we rented were never conducive for a dog and truly we had moved so many times it was probably good we didn't have one. Our overall lifestyle had been extremely unstable. But, now, the dust had settled somewhat and we even managed to rent a beautiful home with a fenced yard! This was a place where we knew we could finally, stay awhile. I felt such relief. The turbulence of our rocky marriage had temporarily subsided and we both felt that the addition of a dog would add a sense of "normalcy"to our family life with our two sons.

We made a trek to the nearest animal shelter and began our search. For me, this was a heartbreaking experience. I wanted to give most of the dogs there a good home. Row after row we observed all the adorable bundles of fur waiting in earnest and hoping that someone, anyone, would snap them up and provide for them a wonderful home. I couldn't help but wonder how they all felt, but I knew how it felt to me. I knew each of these precious creatures had a story. Then it struck me so clearly that the stories didn't matter, as each and every one of them was "God" in a most unique disguise. Yes, it may be an interesting perspective and one that is hard to grasp. But consider just a moment … what if it were true? Saint Francis of Assisi, the patron saint of animals, knew it. He referred to all creations, whether human, or not, as "the face of God."

Most of us have either personally experienced or heard true accounts about a dog saving someone's life. There are documented accounts of dogs that traveled hundreds of miles and even thousands of miles to find their owners after being "separated" from them. Dogs are now even being "called upon" to assist in the healing arts. There have been studies showing that blood pressure can be lowered by the simple act of petting a dog, and, that dogs can actually calm the human nervous system. (Not too shabby, I'd say.) The effects of love without condition are unfathomable to most humans because many times the human mind has many conditions, or as I call it, "agendas." We want others to make us feel good, so this dynamic usually comes in the form of doing things to solicit a desired response. A dog can make us feel better just by its presence. What a concept …"Presence"!

At the animal shelter, as I contemplated these things in my heart, there sat those very "present" adorable creatures. As we passed by cage after cage, I knew that the dog that was to be ours was not there. I knew I had to be patient. As much as I wanted to leave with a dog that day — or a puppy — that was not the reality that played out. But, we just never know what a day can bring. It was summer and there were still plenty of hours of daylight. As we departed, I trusted that each dog there would find that perfect connection, and have an "upgrade" within their lives. Then I let go.

After David and I arrived home, I decided to do some gardening. I never cease to be amazed at how much clarity one can amass from the simple task of pulling a weed or sculpting a bush. Then again, it is not so surprising. Years ago, I read a book that had a phrase in it I will always remember. The phrase is, "Work is love made visible." Could we even fathom in our wildest imaginings a world in which everyone loved their work? The funny thing is, it is not about the work, it is the love. Beautifying the outdoors is not something to be controlled, but rather to create an environment so the essence stands out. We would not need to "do" so much if the love element were present.

When God Wears Fur

David decided he would clean the windows. We lived in a magical house that inspired wonder. The living room had vaulted ceilings with windows along the perimeter. We could actually watch the clouds go by from the comfort of our own living room. We had always rented, and we made this particular property by far our most beautiful home yet. David and I had a way of making every home we lived in sparkle. We, without fail, left each property in much better condition when we moved out than when we found it. We always got our deposit back. However, this home was the first place since we had been married that really felt like "home." It had a welcoming "presence" and spectacular curb appeal.

So, David was high upon an extension ladder cleaning the inside of the windows, and I was digging in the dirt outside. I began hearing a tapping noise. I was looking all around trying to figure out where the noise was originating when I looked up. It was David tapping on the window excitedly and pointing across the street. My back was facing the street so I turned to see why David was trying to get my attention. I could hardly believe my eyes, but there it was. Both David and I were observing what we had wanted to see all day. I could not help but laugh and I thought to myself, "Isn't this just the way life works? We go searching all over for what we all are looking for and the entire time it is in our own back yard," or in this case, our front yard.

There across the street in our neighbor's front yard was the most adorable Sheltie puppy! It was running, barking, and having the best time. Ironically, this was the exact breed I had dreamed of having for a very long time. When we lived in Columbus, Ohio, I had seen one in a pet store. I had wanted so much to buy him, but we had no yard to speak of and it was not fenced. It is most important that things "feel" right, and even though I wanted that dog, it would not have been the best arrangement.

I found myself bolting across the street to our neighbor's front yard. I asked if I could hold the puppy. My neighbor Cindy said, "Yes, but it is not ours." She went on to say that the puppy belonged to some friends of theirs who had stopped by to visit. The new proud owners emerged from Cindy's house and we made introductions. I asked where they had purchased the puppy and if there were any puppies left in that litter. They said they thought there was one male left. Now my head was really spinning. As I examined the events of the day piece by piece, I could not help but see that everything was lining up. There was an invisible force at work. I asked if they had a phone number for the breeder. They said they did and they would call us when they got home that evening. About eight p.m. that night the call came. Finally having the number of the breeder, I found myself more than anxious for the following day. I could hardly wait to call.

The following morning before I sailed out the door for work I placed the call. A soft voice answered with a kind, "Hello." "Hello," I said, "My name is Jane Lí and I am inquiring about a male Sheltie puppy you may have for sale." "Well," the voice on the other end of the phone replied, "I'm afraid he is already spoken for." I could not believe I was hearing this, how could this be? There were so many synchronistic events surrounding this process with this dog, I had a hard time believing it was all for nothing. She then introduced herself, "My name is Marilyn," she said, "...and I've been at this breeding thing for about twenty- two years." She went on to say she had two females left if I was interested. I asked her when she would expect her next litter of puppies. She said that this was the last. She had been doing it long enough. I thanked her for her time, but I knew in my heart that the dog we would own would be a male. She requested my name and phone number, "just in case." I was happy to give it to her, because one thing I do know for sure is that nothing is random in this wonderful universe of ours. Still, as I hung up the phone, my heart sank in disappointment. I had been so sure this was our dog.

Memory is a funny thing ... I found myself in a self-created time capsule that regressed to my childhood, age eight, to be exact. Memories came flooding back of all the times I had wanted a dog but was not allowed to have one. I remembered so clearly on this occasion of wanting a German Shepherd. This was my favorite breed at that age. It may have had to do with a favorite television show that aired back then called, "Rin Tin Tin," in which a German Shepherd starred. They just seemed so intelligent with an essence of royalty, to boot. It also seemed like a German Shepherd would be good for protection. As a child, I believed I needed that.

Then, a most peculiar thing happened. I awoke one school morning, and as I emerged from my bedroom, my mother cornered me and in a very subdued voice said, "Janie, do not go out into the patio. Your stepbrother came home from the Air Force last night and brought a dog with him." Then the tone of her next words she spoke hit me like a lightning bolt. "The dog is vicious and he only likes Chuck, so don't go near him!" "They'll both be gone in a couple of days." I responded inquisitively but quietly, "What kind of dog is it?" With anger as an overlay, the words flew like darts thrown at a target: "It's a German Shepherd!" I could not believe my ears. A German Shepherd was in our very own house! Of course, all I could think of was that I wanted to see him. "Do you know his name?" I asked my mother. As she spoke his name, in some odd way I already knew of his royalty. "King," she said, "His name is King."

As far back as I could remember I have had an affinity for dogs, and, really, all animals. I think some of us are just "made up" that way. I would go so far as to say it might even be in our genetic code. But, one thing was for sure, and that was most of my life I felt more at home with the creatures in furry coats than I did with most of the people with whom I resided.

The next thing I knew I was tiptoeing to the patio door. There was an entrance door that connected to the master bedroom and another door that entered into the living room. Of course, I chose the more secluded route, the bedroom. A sheer cream-colored curtain hung from the top to bottom on a tension rod, as the door was clear glass with the exception of the frame. I gingerly pulled back the curtain just enough so that I could view the "vicious" dog myself. There he was; it was al- most as if he was waiting for me. I know he sensed my presence early on. His name was so appropriate. What I saw was a "King." He approached the door and there we both stood silently as our eyes locked on each other. I was not sure what he saw that day, but what I saw was God in one of his many disguises. As I pen this now, I believe what we were doing was peering into each other's souls.

Ever so carefully, I cupped my small hand around the doorknob and began to turn it as quietly as I could. I opened the door just enough to slip my small frame through. With Chuck still fast asleep on the sofa, King began to lick my hands and face. I was beaming from head to toe. I had the feeling that King was going to be my dog and I was right.

After that encounter, I was able to sneak back in the house without notice. I kept my rendezvous with King to myself and strolled off to school. If there was ever a magical day, this was it. All I could think of was going home and seeing King. It was if my dream had come true and I was really going to have a dog. Of course, none of this had been set in motion, except within the confines of my heart- and, really, that is all it takes. The other pieces of my "perfect picture" then fell in line, so to speak. King was even the breed I had wanted!

Shortly after arriving home from school, King greeted me. He was just as ex- cited to see me, as I was him. My mother was not exactly elated about my newfound friend, but it was very apparent to me that she saw the connection between the two of us. Since she saw that King really liked me, I asked if I could take him out for a walk. Reluctantly, she said it would be all right. She knew how much I had wanted a German Shepherd and the fear was beginning to "seize" her. I was definitely too young to realize the reasons for her fear that I would learn later on. However, for that brief time of innocence, I had a dog to take for a walk. Out we went, just the two of us. I remember the chain leash I attached to the collar as if I had just done it this very day.

I felt such an enormous sense of pride as King and I walked side by side. I wanted the whole world to know that he was my dog. For the next few days, King and I were practically inseparable, and then a most unexpected thing happened. My stepbrother Chuck, King's owner, came by to say he was moving to an apartment and that he could not have a dog there. He asked me if I would like to keep King. Chuck should have asked my parents this question, but instead, of course, *my* answer was, "yes!" I could not believe my ears. King was really going to be my dog.

At my age, I had no idea what the ramifications would be of this situation, and I certainly hadn't any idea of my family's financial dilemma. I do not recall ever even asking my mother and stepfather if I could keep King. I think more or less the scenario went something like this: "Mom, Dad, Chuck said I could have King!" Funny thing was, neither one of them said anything to the contrary, so I think I assumed it was all right.

Knowing my dog King would be there waiting for me, sure made coming home from school *absolutely* delightful! Dogs constantly remind us of how important the "now" moments are. I believe that for a good portion of the time, we are "most present" when we are with animals. They seem to command that, without us even knowing it. Being present with what is before us is imperative for generating a feeling of well being and peacefulness.

Somehow, I recognized early on through experiences I had with King, that I was being taught (or guided) to love and appreciate what was in front of me — but not to "attach" myself to it. If we truly love without condition we can "let go" because we have the confidence we will always have what we need. Dogs, as well as humans, are not possessions to own and sometimes both are only with us for a very short time.

One afternoon as I arrived home, before I even walked in the door I knew something was wrong. I knew King was gone. The silence was so loud it was all consuming in that moment. It felt to me as if someone had died, the space felt that empty! I went from room to room in search of King when I found my mother sitting quietly on the patio. I approached her and with extreme reluctance, I asked the question, "Where's King?" "Janie," she replied, "We got rid of him; we just could not afford to feed him." I may not have had King anymore, but what I did have were some awesomely wonderful memories and I knew one day I would have a dog again, one as special as "King."

So now, years later, here I sat again as an adult, perplexed as to what had happened when I spoke to the Sheltie breeder three days ago, because I felt so impeccably sure this Sheltie was my dog. I found it most interesting that this event sent me light years into the past where I crossed paths with my very first dog, but most definitely, he would not be the last. We just never know what a day may bring. There is the most wonderful thing about the unexpected, and the element of surprise. As a gardener, it's like planting a seed packet of wild flowers. You know something is going to pop up out of the soil, but you're never quite sure what, until it does. I really wanted something phenomenal to happen. Even though it seemed up to this point that things had not gone too favorably, I had always believed the miraculous could occur, and trusted that it would.

As I arrived home on the fourth day since I spoke to Marilyn, the breeder, my first order of business was to check our phone messages. There was only one phone message that day, but sometimes one message can change the course of one's entire universe. The voice on the recording was one I had heard before. "Hello, Jane Lí, this is Marilyn, the Sheltie breeder." The words that came next were almost unbelievable. "I think the Lord wants you to have this puppy! Will you please give me a call?" I could not believe my ears, nor could I dial the numbers fast enough. I must admit that I was overwhelmed with excitement, as the phone rang on the other end. "Hello." "This is Jane Lí." "Oh, yes, Jane Lí, thank you for calling back so soon." She continued, "The man this dog was promised to was on his way to pick him up. Then the oddest thing happened. He called me from a pay phone and said he had changed his mind! He said he didn't even know why! I did not think this so unusual except that this is the second time this has happened with this same dog! This is why I can't help but consider that something larger is at work here and it must be the Lord." Indeed, I felt the same way, and I was so incredibly relieved! All of the pieces were now coming together to create the picture I had dreamed about.

My next question to Marilyn was one we had not discussed, simply because things had not gone that far. "How much is he?" I asked the question with slight hesitation because we were on a pretty tight budget. "Well," Marilyn replied, he is oversized so you will never be able to 'show' him." This was not a problem because I just wanted *this* dog. A show dog had never even entered my mind. "I will give you a discount of fifty dollars because of this, so you can have him for four hundred dollars instead of four hundred fifty." That sure sounded like an awful lot of money simply because we did not have an extra four hundred dollars just lying around for anything- much less a dog. But, what we did have was the commonality of knowing that the events that had transpired up to this point were no coincidence. So, with that being the case, I took a deep breath and said, "Marilyn, we do not have four hundred dollars to purchase this puppy right now." Her response left me speechless but also incredibly grateful. She matter-of-factly blurted out, "That's okay, you can make payments! It's like I said, it's your dog!"

It is an amazing feeling to be trusted, all on its own, but trusted by someone you have never met is even more amazing. I believe we all know whom we can trust if we listen to our own heart and learn to silence the mind. The heart is the higher intelligence and has the capability to "tune in" to what is missed by our "gray matter." Some would call this the subconscious. I personally do not think the label is important. What is important is that we "get it." (Dogs have this one mastered.)

With all the particulars squared away, it seemed that the next order of business was to ask when I could come and pick up the puppy. Marilyn said anytime was fine because he was ready to go. We arranged a time, I got directions, and two days later, I was on the road, making my way to Puyallup, Washington. This was about an hour and forty- five minute drive. As I drove my old gold V8 Plymouth Volaré, I gazed at the box I had placed on the passenger seat. Nothing special, just a small, plain, cardboard box- it was one of the necessary items Marilyn had told me to have in tow. She explained it would make the puppy feel more secure if he was in a box next to me, riding shotgun. She went on to say that, she had had more than one episode involving carsickness, and that Shelties seemed to be prone to it. All of this information was most interesting since I was a novice, a pet-owner-to-be.

I had absolutely no idea what to expect. However, something felt vaguely familiar about this process. Then it hit me, how similar it is to bringing a baby home for the very first time. My husband David and I had done this twice because we had two sons. From this vantage point I began to project the homecoming of this dear sweet puppy I was about to pick up. David and I chose not to tell the boys. We so wanted to surprise them. I began playing out a myriad of scenarios in my head regarding our sons' reactions to our new family member. They both had wanted a dog for a very long time. I had a succinct picture in my mind of what the puppy would look like. The excitement and anticipation was mounting, as I realized I was almost there.

I arrived at what one would term a modest home. Nothing much stood out about it. It was a basic three-bedroom rambler with a fenced yard, situated at the curve of a cul-de-sac. Not much curb appeal, that was for sure, but none of those things mattered because this home housed many faces of "God" in fur coats, just waiting for the opportunity to grace the lives of some folks lucky enough to acquire one, and I was among them. I parked my car and approached the house. I was doing my best to act calm and subdued, but some things you just can't hide no matter what. I took a few deep breaths and rang the doorbell.

A dark-haired, medium framed woman appeared. Her presence was one of kindness. It was evident we were both excited to see the other. "You must be Jane Lí, I'm Marilyn, please come in, come in!" As we looked at each other we were both reassured. Any doubts either of us had about the other were abated. As Marilyn showed me her home and all of her dogs, without question, they were her family, and what a precious sight it was to see. It seems each dog had a story of its own personal uniqueness complete with preferences and quirks. To date she housed twenty-two dogs. What intrigued me was that they all seemed happy and content.

Marilyn had no trouble seeing the anxiousness in my eyes as they scoped the periphery of the room where we stood. I was without a doubt looking at all of the dogs and wondering where the puppy was, my puppy that I had come to retrieve. The anticipation within my heart was now overflowing. Right then as if on cue, Marilyn announced, "Well, let's go find him!" The task was not as easy as one would think. The next words Marilyn spoke took me by surprise. She said, "We gave him the name "Brat" because he is always in the middle of everything!" "Brat," I thought, "what an odd name, and of course we would change it," was my next thought.

After what seemed like forever, Marilyn spotted him behind a large tan overstuffed chair. The moment I laid eyes on him, I recognized having seen this dog before in my "mind's eye." I picked him up and looked directly into his eyes. Small as he was he had a presence about him that could have filled an entire auditorium. In that very moment I realized just what this presence was: "Love without condition." I felt honored and humbled at the same time. Then I thought, "Gosh, there is just so much we take for granted." Time became nonexistent as I basked in the reality that soon I would be exiting with "God in fur." I also was aware that somehow this incredible being would transform our entire family. Little did I know just how right I was.

Needless to say the ride home was a huge relief. I had placed "Brat" in the small box next to me and off we went. Since my car was an automatic I drove with my left hand and kept my right hand on the puppy. I wanted him to have personal contact with me before we arrived home, plus I thought it would be of comfort to him. As the two of us made our way home, I knew in the depths of my heart that I would be eternally grateful for this dear, sweet, brown haired woman named Marilyn. She had no idea I am sure that a new corridor had opened in my heart that day. It was like I had stepped into a new dimension, and there was no turning back.

We arrived home without incident, no throwing up, no whining (the things Marilyn had cautioned me about). "Brat" was "quiet as a church mouse," as they say. Honestly, it felt to me, he was quite relieved to be free of the chaos of living with twenty-one other dogs! I could not wait to take him in the house because I knew David and our two sons, Justin and Jesse, would be home.

I walked in the front door carrying Brat and announced, "Hey everyone, I'm home!" Jesse was the first to come down the stairs. "Hi Mom, cute puppy whose is it?" "Would you like to hold him?" I replied. "Sure," said Jesse. Jesse was seven years old then. It melted my heart to observe Jesse with our new puppy. He was being so careful with him. It reminded me of years past when Jesse was born and watching how careful Justin, his older brother was with him. Then I spoke up and said to Jesse, "He is our dog, we get to keep him!" Jesse's next question caught me off guard, and yet it was the most appropriate timing yielding a profound response within me: "What is his name?" Without any hesitation I said, "Phoenix, his name is Phoenix." Some things in life are just not negotiable, and at that moment when his authentic name left my lips, I knew this was one of them.

It was most definitely a time of celebration in the Fox household. We were all so elated to have this precious little dog under our roof. None of us had a clue about how profound the effects would be of having "God in fur" in our midst. Nor did we have the slightest inkling of how many times our dear little Phoenix would rise from the ashes.

Spanky Li

3

Integration

"Oh, to look into the eyes of our faithful furry friends, and to see the face of God in one of many disguises" – Jane Li

To me, "Integration" is a transformational concept that describes a coming together of a multiplicity of factors that inspire us to want to be a part of a larger whole after a period of feeling separate.

When the sun is shining in Western Washington, the parade is never ending as "God" out on a leash "struts their stuff." The adorable furry faces combined with eyes of love call us to "connect," be it with others or ourselves. Folks who would otherwise not give you the time of day suddenly "notice." Complete strangers stop to talk and situations that on an average day would evade us, now become commonplace. Being an avid animal lover I used to wonder about people who had no interest whatsoever in four-legged beings wearing a fur coat.

There were times in the not so distant past that you'd be hard pressed to find an apartment or rental home that allowed pets. Now, there are even huge signs that read, "Pets Welcome!" You just gotta love it, I certainly do! For many people these days, their dogs are their family. But over the years, I've come to realize that if we have a difficult time connecting with "God in fur," oftentimes it is because we feel a *"disconnect"* within ourselves. We fail to recognize that everything we "observe" is also a part of us. This alone can be very frightening for some.

As two-legged beings walking around with so many "programs" running, about how things "should be," we miss the entire picture of what "is" or can be… mainly, the *miraculous*. But dogs are masters at debunking our so called "realities" and what is most amazing is just how they go about doing it. They do it by being *here now*, in the present moment. I like to refer to this as "The Now Dimension" because in this "now," nothing else matters. Why? Because nothing else exists. Dogs are not spending their energies projecting about future events. They are too busy having a great time *now*.

I love to watch dogs play, especially when it comes to something as simple as "throw and fetch." I have observed a dynamic over and over, which speaks volumes in metaphor to the human race: When a dog brings his ball or toy to someone to engage in play and that person refuses, guess what happens? Without fail, if there are other people around the dog will go somewhere else! Dogs do not create a huge drama around someone who does not wish to play. They are on to the next round of fun wherever that may be with the next person who may want to play. They most definitely have the market cornered at "seizing the moment"!

I know, by now you may be saying to yourself something like, "Well, life is really not this simple, after all we *are* humans, not dogs!" So what I would say to that is, "What usually brings us the most joy?"... The simple things. Simplicity speaks to the heart. Dogs do not compartmentalize life into tiny boxes with bows. They wear their heart on their sleeve, or "paws" rather, for all to see. No holds barred. What's more, I have never really seen a dog that seemed bored doing the same thing over and over because in the now dimension every moment is new. Currently my good friend David (and former husband) has a dog named Chip. He never tires of fetching his toy. Oh, he may take a breather and rest for a bit, but then he is right back at it, "going for broke."

Phoenix gave us a shining example of both the importance of "now" and "simplicity," all rolled into about one hour, on a very hot summer day. Every afternoon we would put Phoenix out in the back yard to do his business and to play for awhile. Oftentimes when we would go to get him, he would be fast asleep under his favorite tree. However, this one day in particular, when I went out to retrieve him, he was gone! On occasion, the side gate would be left open, and we would usually check to make sure it was securely closed. However, this was a day we did not. It was a Saturday afternoon in late August so both David and I were home. David was frantic as he posed the question, "Where do you think he is?" The answer that left my lips came just as clear as the night sky filled with constellations. I replied, "He is with the children." David responded with a tone of urgent concern in his voice, "And just where is that?" Reassuring him, I said, "Let's take a walk around the block." So, off we went, but really, we did not walk, we ran. When we got to the next block, halfway down on someone's front lawn; stood Phoenix with two little girls. We were delighted to be the "observers" as he entertained them both. One of the girls looked to be about seven and the other about five. Phoenix was still a puppy and not very big, but the joy he brought these two girls was grand. It was then I realized that this dog's mission was to spread as much of this joy as possible to all with whom he would come in contact.

I approached the two little girls and explained that the puppy was our dog and that we needed to take him home. The older girl then asked me, "Well, what is his name?" I replied, "Phoenix." Then the younger girl began to giggle and whispered something to the older girl. However, I could hear every word she spoke as she said, "Did you hear that? His name is 'Kleenex'!" We laughed about that incident for years, but the truth is; those words spoken from the lips of that precious little girl were exquisitely accurate. As Phoenix's life unfolded, it became clearer and clearer how much he "absorbed" our family's dysfunction in his attempt to "help" us. This is a big part of what dogs do. They "take on" many of their owner's physical or emotional issues in their own bodies and in some cases, even terminal illness. Their love is so pure and without condition, they will go to the "nth" degree for those they love. This is why they not only deserve our love, but also our honor.

There was no question we loved having Phoenix, and that he loved his new home. At the time we lived in a reasonably quiet neighborhood where most of the streets were lined with tall majestic fir trees in variegated colors of green. Every night unless it was pouring rain, David and I were out walking Phoenix. What started out as just plain exercise became a powerful point of "connection" because as we walked, we talked. Then what began as talking morphed into real communication, at least for the duration of those mini-excursions. The mere "act" of walking our dog, became a magical "drop zone" we entered and connected "heart to heart." As I look back now, I believe that those walks were the sweetest times of our entire marriage, as well as the most calming.

Integration was beginning to take place that was not just one of Phoenix blending with us. His presence was bringing on an element of exploration or "door" to begin to access dimensions within ourselves that we hadn't a clue existed. Our whole family was well on its way to radical changes.

When we begin to recognize "God in fur," we begin to recognize God everywhere and in the most unlikely places. What began as the purchase of a dog was now becoming a road to the infinite.

Coco and Monty

4
From Chaos to Calm
(Phoenix Rising)

"He who has courage and faith will never perish in misery"
— Anne Frank 1929-1945

One of the most challenging things we as pet owners have to deal with are injuries and health issues when they arise. Just like children, our pets need and require our "presence" and care in larger doses until whatever the issue may be has subsided.

Now I know it may be difficult to fathom "God in fur" having an injury or health crisis, but, I've come to believe that these are disguises as well. If we are willing to "shift" our perceptions about what we label as good and bad, sick and healthy, we can leap light years into a place of calm, a "state" of being that "all is well," even in the face of a loved one's passing. Please understand, I am not saying that we will not miss our faithful friends. We in the human form have that trait, whereby we miss our interactions with other forms that have passed on before us.

In contrast, what I am saying is that the apparent disasters, accidents, injuries, illnesses and the like, can have profound and life changing experiences at the center. We all have the ability to live in the "eye of the storm" so to speak, and it is so much easier to do this *if we are not resisting* the storm. There is an ancient quotation that says, "When you look into the ashes, look well." This quote could be interpreted many ways. To me, it speaks of finding the "gold" in the apparent loss, disaster, or illness because it is *always* there. I also realize there is a construct, something we call "time," so we do not always see the "gold" right away. We may feel powerless and get "stuck" in the event that is playing out, instead of moving to a higher plane that perhaps we are being called to embrace. Either way, it is all just fine because love weaves its tapestry through our hearts and eventually we awaken to its call.

Phoenix demonstrated this very dynamic to us many times, and what occurred one late summer night was no exception. It was Saturday night. We had just finished watching an episode of "Saturday Night Live" and we were preparing to retire for the evening. David took Phoenix out to do his usual business. After about ten minutes, I heard the two re-enter the house. One of Phoenix's favorite things was to run down the hallway full speed and jump onto our bed. This was quite a feat because we did not have the average queen sized bed. It was a wooden four-poster, high off the floor model with a head and foot board ornately designed.

I could hear Phoenix running to accomplish his "Olympic like' exercise when the unthinkable happened. One could best describe this as watching a movie in slow motion and feeling completely helpless to stop it. I watched as Phoenix in mid-flight, missed the bed, flipped over backwards, and hit the floor with a resounding thud. I was on the opposite side of the bed when this occurred. But even before I saw him, I knew he was severely injured. As I ran around the bed, there was Phoenix lying quietly. To look at him at first glance, one would never know how badly he was injured. In that moment it was crystal clear to me that Phoenix had entered the next phase of his "sacred mission." As I gathered him up off the floor, I noticed one of his hind legs was just dangling. I knew that not only had the leg been broken but it was also dislocated. As far back as I can remember I have done well in the midst of a crisis, and this time was no different. I may fall apart in the aftermath, but I can handle whatever it is until some form of equilibrium is restored.

David as well as our two sons, Justin and Jesse, were frantic when they saw Phoenix's leg. I, however, remained calm as I began giving instructions matter-of-factly, as it was "business as usual." I asked David to call the emergency vet clinic and inform them of what had happened and that we were on our way. I asked Justin our oldest son to get a blanket to wrap around Phoenix while in transport because it was very clear that he was in shock. Justin then carried Phoenix out to the car, and the rest of us piled into my 1989 Volkswagen Jetta and off we went to the animal "ER." It can be stressful assisting an injured animal, but truly it is much more intense dealing with humans when they are "falling apart at the seams."

What has always carried an air of intrigue to me is how animals seem to "know" instinctively when they require the help of humans. It was so apparent to me when I observed Phoenix during his plight that he was in complete acceptance of what was going on. He exhibited no trace of resistance whatsoever. This in itself was a phenomenal blessing.

The fifteen-minute drive to the vet clinic felt like an eternity as the silence in the car was so loud. However, we arrived without incident and, thankfully, Phoenix was taken right in. There is a lot to be said about injuries that occur in the wee hours of the morning. What this usually translates to is that you will not have to wait long in the emergency room, be it hospital or vet clinic. Of course there are exceptions. But at this moment in time, we were all extremely grateful for the immediate attention.

David, Justin, Jesse, and I waited quietly but nervously for the "news." This was without a doubt one of those times I got to practice "letting go" of any "attachment" I might have to a "desired outcome." This is a key component to living in the "eye of the storm." We must let go of the ideas and the structures we've made up in our minds of how we think things "should be." This alone can create the space for the miraculous to waltz right in through the door, and, when we are *least* expecting it.

About a half an hour passed when the vet appeared donning a grim look. She asked to speak with either David or myself. There was no need for words as I quietly nodded and followed her lead to the exam room in the rear of the clinic. She clipped the x-ray film up so she could show me the damage, but with my medical background I knew exactly what I was observing, and that it did not appear to be good. She began to explain the scenario of what the treatment would involve. The leg was indeed broken and dislocated as well. She went on to say that she could put the leg back in the socket and splint it, but we would then have to see our regular vet and that Phoenix would need surgery. The process she described was called "fusing." Once the leg was fused, Phoenix would have much less movement in his leg and his range of motion would be greatly hindered. This would all be to the tune of $2,500. I thanked her and returned to my family in wait. I explained in detail what the doctor had told me. By this time we were all so exhausted, we just wanted to take our dog and go home. And in about an hour that became a reality. Phoenix was returned to us sporting a bright blue splint on his hind leg. Needless to say we all were ecstatic to have our precious Phoenix back, and that we got to bring him back home that same night.

Sometimes a bed can be the most special and sacred place on earth. This was one of those occasions. After arriving home, Justin and Jesse went off to their beds while David and I gingerly placed Phoenix in our bed so that he would be between the two of us. As I observed Phoenix lying there so peacefully, I traveled back in my mind to the times when our sons were just tiny babies. Many a night they slept between us until they were big enough to sleep in a crib. Odd as it may seem, having dear Phoenix there was no different. He most assuredly was our "family." All was calm now in the Fox household as everyone drifted off to sleep. Everyone that is, except me.

I knew some grand-scale decisions would have to be made the next day regarding Phoenix and his impending "surgery," and I also knew that ultimately it would be up to me to make that call. The biggest concern I had was that I did not want to make a decision from a place of fear. The "what ifs" can be a continual plague if we allow it to overtake us. I "knew" there was another option besides this elaborate surgery. And, that other option without question falls into the category of the miraculous. I felt such an intense conviction in my heart that this was exactly what was "on order" for Phoenix: A Miracle. I asked the unseen world to provide the scenario that would be the best possible outcome for Phoenix, and with that, I closed my eyes in peace. I knew I would have the answer in the morning.

I awoke to the aroma of freshly brewed coffee. After the events of the night before feeling sluggish was a gross understatement. I began to stretch out when I realized with a jolt that Phoenix was next to me! And sure enough, there he was, still sleeping peacefully. Then I remembered the question I had asked before I fell asleep, and suddenly the answer was "downloaded" into my present awareness. Just as clear as day, I heard, "Do not do the surgery!" "Easy for you to say," I thought to myself. Then came the next phrase, "Take him to see the 'Magic Man.'" I know this may sound quite odd, but I knew exactly who this man was. He was an alternative practitioner that was dubbed the "Magic Man" because the people and animals he "treated" seemed to have miraculous results, and sometimes it would be immediate. Quite honestly, he did practice what he preached. He, himself, had a terrible accident when he was young and was told he would never walk again. Apparently, someone was not correct in their diagnosis, because he has been walking fine for years. Which brings up the subject of "realities":

It is easy to look at a circumstance or injury and make a judgment of what you see or even what may "show up" on an x-ray film. But I would challenge a "reality" in which these assumptions, diagnoses, judgments, or whatever label we wish to place on it, are set in stone. Any "reality" is changeable in any given moment. And many times we are not really seeing what we think we see. Being open to the possibility of the impossible occurring is exactly the main ingredient for a miracle.

I made the call to the "Magic Man." The voice on the other end was calming as well as cheerful. I told him what had happened and his response was exactly what I wanted to hear. "Don't worry," he said with unwavering conviction, "he'll be fine. Can you bring him to me tomorrow?" "Of course," I replied with jubilation, "What time?" "About eleven A.M." "See you then," I said, and as I hung up the phone I breathed a huge sigh of relief. I looked at Phoenix and said, "Tomorrow we're going to see the 'Magic Man' and you are going to be fine without surgery." I knew I just had to pass the feeling of reassurance on to Phoenix. But really, I was just reassuring myself because Phoenix was already just fine. After all, this was "God in fur."

Now it was time for the really important issue at hand. We had to take Phoenix out to do his "business." I must admit I had concerns about just how Phoenix would pull this one off. David ever so gently carried Phoenix out to the back yard. It was early spring and because of the torrential rains that year our grass had not been mowed for months. As I looked out the sliding door I thought, "How is he ever going to be able to walk out there, much less go to the bathroom?" As David delicately placed dear Phoenix on the lawn, I began to observe what I would call a dance of "silent wonder." It reminded me of the time I was a small child and my father took me to see the ballet production "Swan Lake." I remembered watching and wondering how they were able to do the moves with such grace and ease.

Watching Phoenix maneuver was no different. I thought to myself, "Why do we ever doubt?" Of course I realized that all of the "concerns" I had made up in my head, were just that. Made up. Phoenix acted as if nothing had happened. This is quite a testimony for us humans. We can repeat our dramas, pains, problems, illnesses, and anger for sometimes years on end before we "let go," and sometimes we never do. And yet here was our precious little dog just happy as can be. It was "business as usual."

Sunday flew by. I could not wait to take him to see the "Magic Man" the following day. David and I had already entertained and discussed the idea that we may still have to do the surgery, but we wanted to give the unseen world first opportunity. We both were in agreement, and on board for a miracle. Monday morning came, and I was excited about the pending possibilities that lay ahead for Phoenix. I had both of us ready, and dear David carried Phoenix out to the car. He could have actually walked himself, but there were some stairs involved and they were not on the menu yet for Phoenix. I had the x-ray film that the vet at the clinic had taken, and off we went. Overall, it was a bit of a jaunt, taking us about forty-five minutes to reach our destination.

I pulled into the dirt parking lot of a Montessori school. This kind gentleman, the "Magic Man," used one of the school's outbuildings to "treat" people and animals. It was a large open room with seating around the periphery. The protocol was to take a seat and wait your turn. So, those of us in wait observed others that were being "treated." It was quite impressive. What I would term a "common thread" is found among folk like this gentleman. That thread is ease coupled with fluidity.

When a true master is at work, there is no struggle. There is only calm, and know-ingness that the answers have "already" arrived. And there is an awareness that ego has no part in, because they know they are only a doorway to facilitate change. This only leaves room for grace, not ego. Jesus himself said, "I am the door." He provided an opening if people were willing to walk through. Nothing has changed in this arena. We have only become more "educated" being taught that miracles have no place in that particular "box" we label "education." The magic exists "outside" of that "box."

It was finally our turn. He did not require placing Phoenix on the exam table, but rather came around to where we were. I handed him the envelope with the x-ray image. He pulled it out and said something like, "yeah, yeah," and returned it to its holder. He said, "Wait here." When he returned he was carrying a small brown paper bag. The bag contained some fine black powder. His instructions were just as simple as the small paper bag, "Give him this twice a day with his food, bring him back in three weeks and we'll remove the splint." I replied, "That's it?" and he said, "Yep, that's it, he'll be fine."

Trust. Now there's a word that doesn't hold much clout in the "real" world. Yet it is precursor to the miraculous. In order to really trust, there can be no remnants of doubt. Dogs are masters at trust. Phoenix, in some odd way, was helping me to remember that reality, and just how powerful flowing with trust really is. Our entire universe is contingent upon trust … Driving home, I knew without a doubt, Phoenix would be walking just fine without a splint in three weeks. I reported the day's events to my family that evening after everyone was home. We all agreed upon that reality of what would come to pass without any "drama" and we "let go."

The weeks flew past. I returned with Phoenix to the "Magic Man." We removed the splint. As Phoenix began to walk, there was a slight limp in his step. But after a couple of minutes past he was walking just fine. He never had the surgery. So, I guess one could say the miraculous had occurred. On the other hand, I cannot help but think that the miraculous is an entire world unto itself. All we have to do is trust and become willing to "see" what is on the other side of the door ….

Tuck

5

The Joy Factor

"A merry heart doeth good like a medicine." — *Proverbs 17:22*

As I pen this chapter, in plain view a greeting card adorns my dresser. It is a picture of a dog with its head protruding out the driver's side of a car window. The caption below reads, "Joy is not in things, it is in us." At first glance, one could think the dog is referring to its own species, but upon closer examination, I believe the dog is addressing an essence that resides in each and everyone of us, but sometimes for various reasons it remains dormant. It is what I refer to as "The Joy Factor."

What I just noticed this very night is that directly above this card hangs a picture entitled "Levitation." What washed over me in this moment was a "reality" I have embodied for quite some time. That reality is simply this: In order to see what "God in fur" sees, we must "raise" our consciousness to a new and higher level which will enable us to "see." It is sight that has nothing to do with the physical eye whatso-ever. One could call it "inner vision."

Joy is an "inside job." It emanates from the heart, much like a fountain with an endless supply, that keeps bubbling up to the surface. It is so effervescent that it cannot be contained. This is what God in a fur coat is all about. Joy. What's more, "God in fur" does not need anything outside of itself to experience this feeling of joy. It oozes out of every pore on its body. Believe it or not, joy puts our lives to music and the song just gets sweeter. When joy fills our hearts we not only enjoy the moment but we also look forward to the days ahead, much like a child awaits Christmas Day. I know this may sound a bit over the top to actually live this way, or perhaps it may even be difficult to imagine at all. That's okay because guess what? All we have to do is be open to the possibility of the impossible. This is exactly why our furry friends are here, to remind us that life is meant to be joyful and fun. More and more we are hearing stories of people who have been diagnosed with some dreaded disease and somehow or other they got happy and the ailment magically disappeared. When true joy is combined with love without condition, there is no room for much else except more of the same. Because the expanse of joy is so magnanimous, there *is* only room for more joy, more fun and more love. Ah, what a life!

During the three weeks that Phoenix was sporting his bright blue splint (actually it was a bright blue vet wrap covering the splint), he was called to embark on a rather sacred and important mission. We had an elderly friend whose name was Mr. Hales. He owned the home and pasture that was occupied by my horse, Prince. This gentleman was ninety-one years of age and not in the best of health. I would from time to time take Phoenix to the barn with me. Mr. Hales' side door faced the pasture, which gave him a bird's eye view of the entire "goings on." The pasture was quite large which meant there was lots of room to play. Of course, "play" is probably the most essential ingredient of "The Joy Factor." It is an extension of the bubbling fountain. Besides, there is no end to the fun that one can conjure up within the confines of a horse pasture, especially when you add the magical element of a dog.

As soon as I would arrive at the barn, my first order of business was to feed my horse. Then while he was munching his morning Wheaties which came in the form of Timothy hay and a bit of grain, Phoenix and I would play ball. He never tired of chasing, catching, and returning it. At times, we would forget the ball and chase each other. Now what all this translates to is a spectacular entertainment for our elderly friend, Mr. Hales. He loved my horse Prince, no doubt, but I knew he really looked forward to the times Phoenix accompanied me. So, back to the sacred mission:

One morning I received a phone call from one of the neighbors who lived two houses away from Mr. Hales. I was told that Mr. Hales had taken a terrible fall. He had been lying on his bathroom floor for two days unconscious, before this neighbor had found him. The caller went on to explain what hospital he had been taken to and that his present condition, to be brutally honest, wasn't sounding too hopeful. Of course, the first place I went to was within my heart. Now I knew I had the perfect antidote. I would visit dear Mr. Hales and bring Phoenix, God in a fur coat. So, after placing a call to the facility to inquire about visiting hours, my husband, David, I, and our beloved Phoenix, splint and all, were off to see Mr. Hales. The hospital was only about ten minutes from our home. What was so interesting to me as I observed Phoenix, was I realized he "knew" exactly what we were going to do and why. This is the same "knowing" that makes a dog sit and wait by the door at the exact same time each night, because it knows its master is on the way home.

When we arrived at the hospital we parked the car close to the entrance so dear Phoenix would not have far to walk. The stares from people as we strolled by were nothing short of sheer amazement. Here was this precious little dog hobbling along but doing it with the determination of a racehorse heading towards the finish line. I found my eyes welling up with tears as the three of us entered the hospital. I was honored to be in the "presence" of this kind of love. Once inside, the stares increased of course, because there were even more people. As the three of us made our way through the halls to Mr. Hales' room, we continued to have an audience of folks who clearly could not believe their eyes.

I couldn't help but remind myself in this moment of the intricacies that were being woven in this tapestry of love. It was a pattern of love that reached far beyond anything a human mind could conceive. Yet, here we were as the "observers" or "witnesses" to a Divine plan in the making. Even now as I reminisce to that particular day, I find myself on the verge of tears, not because I feel sadness, but rather a deep sense of honor and recognition for having known such an incredible being with such selfless love.

As soon as we entered the room Mr. Hales was occupying, the fun began. The smile on this man's face could have lit the entire planet. He most assuredly was not expecting to see dear Phoenix. The element of surprise can be most powerful and has the potential to facilitate great change. As the onlookers, it was obvious to both David and me a profound "shift" had occurred within the soul of our dear friend, Mr. Hales. A little bit of joy goes a long way, especially when its wrappings are dressed in fur.

People kept popping into the room as word spread quickly of the adorable dog sporting a bright blue splint. I was halfway tempted to just start taking him room to room because of "The Joy Factor" and wanting to create even more smiles, but for the time and situation it would not have been appropriate.

David gathered Phoenix and put him on the bed next to Mr. Hales so that he could easily pet him. Shortly afterward, the most amazing thing happened. David left the room for a bit and when he did, Mr. Hales motioned to me to come closer. He then asked me something that caught me completely off guard. He asked me if our family would come live with him. He certainly had a large enough home, not to mention that my horse already lived in his pasture. I responded by saying I would have to talk it over with David. I was deeply moved that this kind gentleman would make such a generous offer. However, sometimes what we may "think" is a fantastic opportunity is really not the best thing for us, and we need to examine it more closely. Mr. Hales did not want to leave his home and he knew that because of what had happened he could no longer live alone. I knew he was feeling as though his options were few. I assured him that something would work out and that I would give him an answer in a couple of days.

Meanwhile, Phoenix's presence was working his magic. I felt completely confident that Mr. Hales would recover and return to his home after arrangements were made for added assistance. My husband David and I did in fact discuss the option of moving in with Mr. Hales but at the time our youngest son, Jesse, was a teenager, and played an electric guitar … not exactly a good fit for a man in his nineties! When we told Mr. Hales it just would not be the best thing for all concerned, he understood, and honestly, I think he was relieved. I believe he realized that he was grabbing for a quick solution. Dear Phoenix, however, had played a major role in this man's well being. Mr. Hales did return home. As for myself, I continued to see the importance of love without condition; and how imperative it is in any type of healing.

One of the greatest factors that comes into play with "therapy" dogs is that they have no "judgments," or labels about what the "diagnosis" is, or "story" that is being generated. What's more, is that "God in fur" does not even "see" a problem! It is we humans that tend to focus on the problems, labels, diagnosis and all the details of the so-called illness until we make it "solid" in our mind. This dynamic creates a "reality" that can seem impossible to change. Yet, the miraculous is always waiting behind the next door, if we are willing to open it. Is this not what Christ did? I would venture to say that not many healings or miracles would have occurred if Christ bought into the "problems."

When love without condition is present, healing can happen in an instant. It does not have to take weeks, months, or years. We are never meant to suffer or linger in grief. We are meant to experience joy to its fullest in every capacity of our lives. Joy is not something we learn to do. Joy is what we are.

We may have allowed ourselves to feel too burdened. Or, we may believe that joy is nothing but mere "child's play," and that, "… after all, are we not adults, and isn't life supposed to be serious? … and what about the multitude of responsibilities and duties we have to perform?" I say nay, quite the contrary. However, if you who are reading this find yourself in this category or pattern of thought, I would encourage you to have a conversation with your dog, or if not yours, any friendly dog will do. You may just discover that the dog will appear to be listening intently to your woes, but more than likely its tail will be wagging.

Spencer

6
The Present of Presence

"When we live in the NOW, the door is always open to the miraculous."
—Jane Lí

Of all the animals that reside on this beautiful blue planet we call "Earth," I would venture to say that dogs may have the market cornered when it comes to loyalty. They will stick by their masters through thick and thin, rain or shine, sickness or health, and still have something to contribute at the end of the day.

Phoenix demonstrated this quality of loyalty more times than I could ever catalog. One of the things I would find most astonishing was how Phoenix would react when our oldest son Justin returned home long after he had moved away. From time to time Justin would drop in for a visit, a meal, or perhaps a brief "hello." What became profoundly clear to me was that even before Justin had an opportunity to ring the doorbell, Phoenix knew he had arrived. The excitement Phoenix generated was at times, beyond belief. He would actually "howl" with delight when Justin would enter our home. This action alone spoke volumes to me in regards to love without condition or agenda. In order for this type of elation to come into play, there cannot be one iota of judgment, which also could include the passage of time.

We in human form can be accusative, hostile and even "shun" those who we have decided have not come around or contacted us in a timely fashion. We tend to create these "made up rules" about how certain people "should" behave and then if they do not meet our so-called expectations there's hell to pay, so to speak. We especially like to do this with family members because after all, they are "family," and should know better.

Isn't it curious that dogs behave exactly the opposite? "God in fur" is always overjoyed to see those they love. The time factor is never an issue whatsoever with a dog and why should it be? The present moment is all any of us have. The past is just a series of old stories no matter how dismal or great they can sound. If we are completely and unequivocally honest with ourselves, we know we do not have to prove our worthiness in order for our dog to enjoy loving us. Dogs do not live in the past. Only we humans attempt to do so, which pulls us apart at so many levels. In order to be truly present it is imperative that we be "current," which translates to "NOW." Yes, I know this may seem so much easier said, than done, but so what? There's no time like the present to begin. It does get easier, but we must begin.

In the latter part of winter of the year 2008, I went to visit a friend whom I had not seen in about ten years. She resides in a magical house in Western Washington, heavily surrounded by beautiful, tall, aged evergreens. The home itself stands in a clearing so that when the sun is shining it casts an unusual and mystical glow on her property and everything "sparkles."

This particular day as I made my way up the long dirt road toward her home my eyes caught a sign to the right of the drive that read: "Caution: Deaf Dog." Immediately my mind flashed back ten years prior, when it hit me: "Could this be her adorable dog Sasha?" Then the next thought was, "Oh my gosh, could she still be living?" As I rounded the last turn, my heart smiled as I observed her lovely home. It looked pretty much how I had last remembered it. One could say it was a home that existed in a parallel reality. Not only does it exude a sense of calm and serenity but the overall feeling is one of timelessness. Ah yes, a very important factor to living in the present moment.

I parked my car and as I got out I took a deep breath. It felt like home to me. I stepped up slowly onto the wrap around porch and was about to ring the doorbell when I noticed an adorable gray and white cat who appeared to be the guardian. It sat on its little bed watching ever so intently. I felt like I needed to be granted permission by this cat in order to enter the forbidden territory. So I acknowledged its presence by saying, "Good morning, little kitty cat!" No sooner had I spoken those words, than access had been granted. I rang the bell and there in the doorway was my friend Susanne, much like I had remembered her. She dons a smile that could easily melt an iceberg. Then my eyes immediately dropped to the form that was standing about two feet behind my friend.

There she was as I had suspected, dear sweet Sasha. I was so moved in this moment, I could have cried. My friend then broke the silence of our connection to inform me that Sasha was deaf. However, I did not see a deaf dog. What I did see, as well as felt, was an incredibly large, loving presence. I really felt the love. It was literally oozing out of this being like hot lava pouring from a volcano. I bent down and outstretched my hand to her. She approached me ever so slowly and began to lick my hand. I knew the moment we made eye contact, she remembered me. It was as if she was saying, "Welcome Home," which is completely apropos because love recognizes itself. It is these type of occurrences that enable us to "tune in" to the timelessness of love. Love without condition has no consciousness of time. Whether its ten days or ten years, nothing ever changes in the essence of this kind of love.

So what does it really mean to be present? In contrast, I would say simply to ask yourself if you've ever been with someone else, but felt utterly and completely alone. Most likely that person or persons were not really "there" in terms of focus and attention. They could have been off in a whole other world. Meanwhile, we could have been thinking we were having a great conversation, then, when it was time for a response, there was none. We have all experienced this from time to time and no doubt have done this ourselves, on more than one occasion, I am sure. The point is: How do you feel when this happens?

The emotions could range anywhere from feeling ignored, to getting just plain angry. One may even feel outrage that someone would not give attention or want to listen to him or her. Here's the thing: When we are truly "present," words are not even necessary. Dogs are masters at this. I know this may sound a bit "cosmic," but think about it. Dogs do not speak in terms of language as we know it. They don't have to because their "presence" is so enormous! Their signals and transmitters are not being blocked by all the agendas that we humans entertain at times.

Dogs know and understand the language of the heart as this is all that is really needed because everything is contained within that module of love. This is one of the reasons our furry friends are so intensely missed when they are no longer with us. Being present creates expansion. Presence pushes the envelope to a point where it cannot be contained any longer so either things have to shift quickly, or just plain explode, or implode; whatever the case may be. I liken this to lighting a candle in a dark room. The light is so intense the darkness just goes.

I loved the movie "Marley and Me." Marley's owners tried to put him in a "box" of how they thought a dog should behave. But alas, presence had its say because his owners finally "expanded" enough to see that the "box" was not an option for Marley. Acceptance and love prevailed. What came next was fun and magic. Isn't it one of the best feelings ever when someone or something just gets who we are and we don't have to explain or jump through numerous hoops in order to gain love and recognition? There is just nothing like having or being in a relationship where we can be ourselves. No holds barred, just pure unadulterated love, presence, and acceptance. Isn't this truly all we ultimately want? This sounds like a mission for …"God in fur"!

Believe it or not, I was invited and attended a doggie birthday party. It was the first time I had seen such a fabulous parade of fur and fun all in one small, quaint and extremely charming home in Seattle. The party came complete with doggie cupcakes, Hors d'Oeuvres, and pastries that looked exactly like one would see in a fine European bakery. The hostess even had to label them so that the people wouldn't partake of the delicately decorated treats. However, there are still those folks that do not pay attention to signage. While chatting with a friend I noticed a teenager attempting to bite into one of the hard doggie doughnuts. I must admit it was nothing less than hilarious watching this young man's attempt at eating the dog treat. I walked over to him and informed him that what he was trying to eat was in fact, for the dogs. He was horrified and yelled, "Are you kidding me?" and ran off to the bathroom at lightning speed.

Meanwhile God in fur was having the time of its life. There were about seventeen or eighteen dogs that came to play. Monte, the birthday boy as well as the guest of honor, knew exactly what was going on. It was delightful to see all of the dogs getting along splendidly and having oodles of fun. As each new dog arrived with its owner, I watched how the other dogs greeted them. What I "saw" is not easy to describe, because, really, it is beyond words. What I realized in that very moment is that the greatest gift we can ever give ourselves or anyone else is our "presence." I am not only referring to "bodily" presence, because we can be physically present and not be there at all.

Presence is an energetic connection that can only be felt when genuine love is present. It is an "activation," if you will, of something called, "adamantine particles." These particles (not visible to the naked eye) are literally "summoned" into being and multiply exponentially. This is why love without condition attracts more of the same to itself. This kind of "purity" in our love can open doors to entirely new universes of possibility we could never have imagined. This also creates the "presence' so that we can easily "tune in' to what is needed in each, and every moment. It breaks open the boxes and opens our hearts to the infinite possibilities. This could be called "the realm of the miraculous."

A very good friend of mine has a relative who is a certain type of "Christian." This person told my friend that they believed miracles only occur once every one hundred years! This whatsoever did not surprise me; because I "knew" that this was this person's "reality" or "box"! So, in that reality there are no miracles. So, guess what? That person does not see any. Chances are this dear soul may not live to be one hundred years of age and even if they did, they probably would not recognize it as a miracle because it is not in their "box." Most of us have more "boxes" than we could ever catalog. This is why becoming "present" is paramount to being able to step outside of our box, because the "presence" shines the light to help us recognize we are in a box! Yet, this is incredibly simple. A little willingness can go a very long way.

On an energetic level this is what I was observing that bright sunny day as a guest at Monte's birthday party. The doggy birthday party was a smashing success. It was a vehicle of transformation for all who were present that day. All of the dogs were in complete acceptance of each other and were having the time of their lives. As for me, I relished the fact that they were being "recognized." They were no different than we humans. They love parties too.

For years in our family when there was a birthday party, it of course included a birthday cake. An interesting and fun dynamic took place with Phoenix. As soon as I would begin to remove the cake from the box and start placing candles on it, Phoenix would start barking. What I soon realized was Phoenix was singing "Happy Birthday." He recognized that my action was a precursor to what was going to be a joyous celebration and he was already "tuned in" to that reality.

Phoenix would do a similar thing on Christmas Day. He would sit very quiet and patient while we opened our gifts because he knew there were gifts for him as well. But he was fine waiting for his turn. The look in his eyes was one of sheer delight as we said, "Okay Phoenix, it's time for your gifts." We would place them in front of him and he would begin to sniff them. Of course, most of them were edible gifts, but there was always at least one toy for him. He had quite a collection of toys, although his favorite (you may have guessed it) was the ball. His second favorite were toys that would squeak.

Hopefully by now, the picture is coming into focus regarding the example that "God in fur" sets for us. Life is supposed to be fun. This one thing is perhaps in my opinion the greatest reason "God in fur" showed up in the first place. Our friends we call our dogs are nudging us into remembrance. We in our grown up state sometimes forget how to have fun because we are so busy being serious and "stressing" over meaningless issues. These days there are more and more people out walking their dog while talking on their cell phones.

One day as I was working at one of my landscaping accounts, a woman and her dog passed by on the sidewalk. I cannot let a dog go by without saying hello and asking the owner if I might pet their dog. Most folks are fine with it and are appreciative I am noticing their bundle of fur. I approached this lady and her dog and asked if I might pet it. As I did this, the dog told me it was thirsty. So I asked the lady if her dog might be thirsty. She said "YES!" and she was also sort of lost, she said, because she was just not sure where her brother's house was. So, I told her to wait there with her dog while I went to get a bucket of water. When I returned with the bucket in hand, she said actually it was her brother's dog and because she lost her way, the two of them had walked about four miles! The dog lapped up quite a bit of water when the woman said, "I hope I can find my way back to my brother's house." I bent down and said to the dog, whose name was Matilda, "Matilda, take your friend home, because you know the way." I arose and said to this precious soul, "Matilda will take you home, she knows the way." I am sure that all was well in that story. Our dogs are talking to us … are we *listening*?

What if we decided to take ourselves out of our self created boxes? And what if we turned off the TV? What if we decided to "tune in" to a reality of "presence" and "celebration"?

And what if we chose to "show up" for the party?

I think it would be safe to assume there would be no need for gifts, simply because *we* are the "present."

Wally

7
And The Blind Were Made To See

"What the mind is not willing to see, the heart will make manifest" — Jane Li

"A loving person lives in a loving world, a hostile person lives in a hostile world, everyone you meet is your mirror." — Ken Keyes, Jr. 1921-1995

I have come to believe that the most important mission or purpose, of God disguised in fur is to show us humans the aspects of ourselves that if observed, can easily be transmuted with the presence of love.

It is as if they are holding up a mirror and gently asking us to "take a look." No pressure. No judgment. I am hopeful that those of us in the human form are beginning to acknowledge this because this one aspect alone when we "get it" has the potential to change our entire world.

Everything is made up of energy and information, as I stated in a previous chapter, therefore I believe it is safe to say that everything mixes with everything else. We all breathe each other's air; do we not? We also share the same germs; which nowadays for a lot of people can be extremely unnerving.

What I am about to convey may be met with great resistance to the linear mind, nonetheless, it needs to be written. My hope is that many hearts will be illuminated, and change will occur in a most magnanimous way.

As mentioned earlier, our animals energetically, can, and do take on a good portion of their owner's issues. Because of the loyalty aspect of dogs, they are more prone to do this than cats. Cats can be more detached than dogs simply because of their make up. This is not to say that cats will not "take on" issues. Many times they do, as well.

What I have been finding most curious is that dogs nowadays are on the same medications prescribed for humans. These include antidepressants, blood pressure, and pain medications. This alone should pose a huge red flag for us to begin to scratch our heads and wonder, "what is going on?"

Another interesting dynamic I have been noticing is how many people now are reporting their pets missing and/or dying for no apparent reason. The scenarios I have heard quite frequently is this: The cat stops eating. The owners whisk them off to the vet where they are put under observation, and tests are run. Nothing definitive shows up. Cat goes home. Cat still doesn't eat, and within a few weeks the cat expires. This is very curious.

Also, I have been around quite a few dogs lately that are extremely neurotic, anxious, and overall not really happy. Then I observe the owner, and it all makes sense. I was at someone's home where the owner was so extremely controlling that the dog was hiding every chance it got. The answers and solutions can be quite simple if we have eyes to see and ears to hear. But what has been occurring is we have allowed our minds to become so infiltrated with so much energetic "junk" that we have been "attracting" to ourselves many unwanted things, unbeknownst to us, that also effects our pets.

Everything in our universe has a "vibrational" quality or "frequency" that will "attract" to itself "like" frequencies. One could say this is why money attracts money, loving people attract loving people, fear will attract more fear. By now I am sure you have the picture. So, what are we really up to here on planet Earth? We are "awakening": *awakening* to what? Love without condition. Although sometimes the awakening process can be rather painful, it doesn't have to be. It's just that when we put ourselves through what appears to be extreme measures, after a while we tire of the struggle and we let go (*by the way… this is when miracles* **usually** *happen*).

For me, it was wishing to die one Saturday morning at age thirty-four, and literally two hours later I was in a near-fatal car accident. Be careful what you wish for because "thoughts are things." Thoughts create. Realizing this, will help lay the groundwork for thriving during what I know to be one of the most powerful times here on earth. We have the ability to do things a whole lot differently if we decide to.

Things are shifting now at warp speed. You may have noticed certain things that used to work quite well do not seem to any longer. Relationships we once thought were so "right" for us may have lost their "juice." If, however we can decide to just "go with the flow," (by accepting the present moment as it is), life can be an amazing magical experience in which everything somehow works without much effort on our part whatsoever. However, I must warn you that the "flip" side of this can be futile.

When God Wears Fur

A tiny bit of resistance goes a very long way. Resistance to what? Going with the flow. Whenever we attempt to interrupt flow by putting up "energetic" blocks of resistance, we create all kinds of unwanted things in our "reality." Don't worry if this all sounds foreign right now, as at the end of this book there are further references that can assist with clarifying this awareness.

Now to continue with an example of the very thing that may speak volumes to your heart facilitated by "God" in a fur coat holding up a mirror:

When my former husband David and I were still together, some health issues began to surface in David's physical body. He began growing what the medical profession calls "lypomas." These are somewhat hard fatty tumors (usually benign) but they can grow quite large and are unsightly (not to mention it is not much fun to be growing things on one's body). They can, however, be surgically removed.

A few years passed and guess who else began growing these tumors? Phoenix. One showed up on his right shoulder, and grew to be quite large; so much so, that it became necessary to have it removed because it was affecting his ability to walk. The surgery was quite an ordeal especially because Phoenix was already thirteen years old. But being Phoenix, he came through with flying colors. Post-surgery the vet informed us that the tumor weighed two and one half pounds! Now here is the interesting part, no one really knows what causes them or what makes them grow so large. Of course, my response is to look for the solutions and/or answers outside the box. Focusing on a "problem" will *never* bring about the solution; it only makes the problem bigger. I'll discuss this more in the last chapter of the book.

For a while, Phoenix appeared to be doing quite well. It seemed the surgery had given him a new lease on life. It truly was a miraculous recovery for a dog of thirteen years. However, about three years later, after Phoenix had gone to live with David, another lypoma began to grow on his back. It continued to grow in a similar manner as the one we had removed from his shoulder. This was no surprise to me whatsoever because once again he was back in the "morphic field" where lypomas existed. It was at this point I knew dear Phoenix would not be with us much longer.

As absurd as this may seem, this beloved dog named Phoenix had been attempting to show David what he had been holding on to. He was holding up the mirror for David to see himself if he chose to look. By now, it should be crystal clear why this is God showing up in a fur coat. This is love without condition in manifestation. Yet we still may choose not to "see." As a result, many times things may seem to become even more drastic before we are willing to let go.

Phoenix's last important mission was in the making. Little did David realize that this one last effort of our beloved dog would change his life forever. One night after David had returned home from work he took Phoenix out to do his business and go for their usual short walk around the apartment complex. As David reported this event to me he was clearly in disbelief. He said Phoenix just kept wanting to walk. This was very unusual because at this point it was a challenge for Phoenix to even make it around the complex, let alone five or six blocks. But as David stated, "I just allowed him to walk." He said it was as if Phoenix knew exactly where he was going and that he was most definitely on a mission. David followed his lead. Very smart. He led David to a nearby neighborhood that was not far from where David and I had lived just prior to our separation. As David and Phoenix rounded a corner, David's eye caught a moving van. There were people unloading it, and as David and Phoenix approached the van, a woman asked David if he would be willing to help unload a heavy piece of furniture. David replied, "Sure, if you will hold my dog," and he handed her the leash.

That was the beginning of a most tumultuous relationship that would eventually land David in the emergency room fighting for his life. Phoenix "knew" that David was still not "seeing." He had still not awakened enough to realize how dear Phoenix had been selflessly trying to be a mirror for David to "see himself." Phoenix also knew he would be leaving soon, so he literally led David to his next mirror and introduced the two of them.

For a while, it was life in the fast lane until things came crashing down. The relationship did not last long; some things don't have to. I received a call from David one afternoon asking me if I would drive him to see the doctor. He said he was unable to drive himself, because he was too ill. I said I would be happy to. When I arrived at David's apartment and saw him, I asked him if I could just take him to the hospital because I saw blood on the floor. He said "no," so off we went to the doctor's office. Within two hours, we were indeed sitting in the emergency room of a nearby hospital. The doctor had said David needed to be seen immediately. At this point David was knocking at death's door. Neither of us realized he was just a few hours away from expiring.

David was admitted and put in the Intensive Care Unit immediately. For three days, stabilizing David had not been a reality, and no one knew if he was going to make it, David included. Oddly enough, there was a presiding peace I felt throughout the entire ordeal. Miraculously on the fourth day something shifted and they were able to stabilize David. About a week later, David went home.

When God Wears Fur

By the time all of these events of David's had transpired, Phoenix had already been gone two months. With the completion of his final mission, he was finished here on planet Earth. What I found to be interesting is that Phoenix had been hemorrhaging internally when David and I decided to have him put to sleep. Both times when I arrived at David's apartment (on Phoenix's last night and, on the day David went to the hospital), there had been blood on the floor. Coincidence? I think not.

We are undeniably connected to everything around us. Having said this we cannot be forced to awaken to a new reality. The process is similar to when we go to sleep at night. We wake up when we are ready, and sometimes it is abrupt. The greatest factor I know of, however, that helps speed this process along is that of love without condition.

This has not been the easiest chapter for me to write. In closing, I am reminded of the words in one of the most famous songs of our time, "Amazing Grace": "… I once was lost but now am found, was blind but now I see …."

Having said this, by design we were meant to "see," but it is love without condition that opens our "eyes."

Vernon "Blue"

8
Phoenix Returns

"That which we love never perishes; but rather rearranges itself in forms we can recognize and relate to…"

- Jane Li 2009

Many viewpoints, theories, ideas, as well as "channelings" have been circulating for millennia in reference to life after death. Therefore, I feel completely justified stating my ideas as well.

Life, first and foremost, is a continuum. Everything physical without exception began as an idea or thought, before it showed up in manifested form. Another way of saying this is simply that everything is energy and information. It is the arrangement of molecules, atoms, electrons, bozons, and so on, which is responsible for the differences we see between, say, a car and a motorcycle. But it is all made up of the same cosmic "stuff."

From this stance, one could say that really and truly there is no death. It is the rearrangement of energy, perhaps; but no actual death because one cannot "kill" energy and it cannot die. As I stated earlier in this book, we do miss the physical forms when they change and rearrange simply because this goes along with being in human form. However, nothing really ever goes anywhere. This may be difficult to wrap one's head around, so just be open to the possibility and see what shows up.

About a week after we had our beloved Phoenix put to sleep, I was walking in the downtown area of Edmonds, Washington. My destination was the bakery to retrieve a delectable fruit pie for a friend's birthday. Next to the bakery was a toy store which I passed first. So as I strolled past the toy store I was drawn to the "stuffed" animals adorning the glass enclosure.

Whoever originally came up with the idea of stuffed animals was a genius in my book. Perhaps it was derived from the art of the taxidermy; I don't really know. What I do know is that these "stuffed" creations have helped in bringing more joy and delight to millions of folks, both young and old. They are an item that will, in my opinion, never be outdated because they are timeless. Lately, I was introduced to ones that are even breathing as they sleep!

As I continued peering through the window in wonder at all of the varieties, shapes, and sizes of animals, just as clear as the glass I was observing, I heard a faint little whisper that said, "Look for the Sheltie." Since having this type of information floating in was not foreign to me, I began scouring the terrain even more closely but to no avail. There was no stuffed Sheltie in the window. I then decided to go inside and continue my search. There were at least four more shelves inside this store jam packed. I could not recall ever having seen this many stuffed animals all in one space. To say I was delighted, was a gross understatement. Then I saw it! I was dumbfounded and somewhat in disbelief, and amazed, all at the same time. There was the Sheltie. It was as if he was saying, "Here I am, what took you so long?"

There he was, just one amidst all the other animals. As I hurriedly pulled him off the shelf, I noticed his markings were exactly the same, as Phoenix's! What's more is that the dog looked just like Phoenix had as a puppy! But it was when I looked into the eyes that I was "sold." The eyes had a twinkle. This "stuffed" animal actually had a very powerful presence! So, I whisked him up to the counter, paid for him, and off I went, carrying him under my left arm. I was ecstatic with joy of this fabulous find.

Now things began to get most curious. I went to the bakery, picked up the pie, and began my trek back to the car. It was a beautiful sunny afternoon and there were lots of pedestrians since it was the kind of day to be out and about. One after another, people stopped me, wanting to pet my dog! Before I could answer, they were already outstretching their hand to touch the stuffed dog. Then, at the last second a look of surprise would come over them as they would say, "Oh, I thought that was a "real" dog.

I arrived at a crosswalk and as I crossed the street I noticed I was walking toward a little girl with what looked like to be her grandmother. The child pointed to my stuffed dog and yelled, "Puppy, puppy!" The older lady asked me if the child could pet my dog. "Of course," I said with covert excitement. I bent down with the "puppy" and the little girl beamed with delight as she stroked him. As for me, well, it felt as though Phoenix had returned, and the magic continued. I began taking my stuffed dog everywhere: airports, grocery stores, workshops, you name it. The upside of Phoenix being in stuffed form was that there were no vet bills, no food to buy, no poop to scoop, no grooming; just pure fun and freedom.

When God Wears Fur

One of the most profound events that occurred was on Christmas Day of the year 2006. I was invited to a friend's home for food and cocktails in the afternoon. There were many people invited to this joyous celebration. One guest in particular was an elderly woman we'll call "Helen." She was about ninety two years of age at the time and was labeled as having "Alzheimer's." She was sitting in a wheelchair and had been unresponsive for quite some time. As I entered the dining room filled with people, I plopped Phoenix (now in stuffed dog form) down on the table for everyone to see and took a seat. Then a most amazing thing happened. Helen would not take her eyes off my dog. After staring quite intently she asked, "Is that a real dog?" All eyes turned to Helen because…SHE WAS TALKING! My response was just about as shocking as I replied, "Well, **I** think it is." Another question came: "Is it a boy or a girl?" I lifted up the dog and scanned its underside, then said, "I think it's a boy."

Meanwhile the other folks present didn't know what was going on or how to respond, mostly because "Helen" was actually being responsive and conversing with me. Now it was time for me to ask "Helen" a question, so I inquired in a way that made her slip into deep contemplation. I asked her if she would like to have a dog like mine. There was silence for what seemed to be quite awhile, but in truth it may have only been three to five minutes. Her response was remarkable to me. She asked, "Do you think it would be hard to take care of?" I replied, "No, not at all, Helen." I let her son know that I would be ordering a dog like mine from the toy store for his mother. He then informed me that she would probably not remember a thing about it the next day. Somehow that just did not matter to me. What did matter however, was the wonderful presence my "unreal" dog had brought to this dear lady named "Helen," and in turn she was "brought back" from wherever she had been, at least for a time.

The following week I called the toy store and ordered a dog like mine for "Helen." I was told they would contact me when it arrived. It took about one week. I couldn't wait to pick it up and deliver it to "Helen." I had noticed that on previous occasions when I would see stuffed animals that appeared the same breed, that somehow they would each have their own persona. Sometimes I have been known to line up a whole row of say, teddy bears, and carefully scrutinize each face before choosing one. I know this may sound absurd, but each one really has its own unique "energetic signature."

I must admit, the day I arrived to pick up the dog for "Helen," I was quite disappointed. The toy store had ordered two in for me. It was great that I had two choices; however, neither of the dogs had the "Wow" factor that I had experienced when I first saw my stuffed dog, "Phoenix." They had nowhere near the "presence" that Phoenix displayed. Actually, I should have not been surprised whatsoever because on the day I found "Phoenix," I have no doubt that the non-physical Phoenix (that had left his body behind) was guiding me to that particular stuffed dog.

I purchased one of the stuffed Shelties and took it to "Helen's" son's house. He said he would be sure that she received it. I never heard after that what or if anything unusual had transpired, but it really was not important to me. Oftentimes just one simple act of kindness emanating from the heart can change someone's entire world. I know for myself, I will never forget that day of Christmas 2006 when "Helen" came "alive."

One of my favorite quotes originated from my former husband, David. The quote is, "You just never know what a day may bring." As I pen these lines, to date, David and I have been separated for about four and a half years. Nonetheless, we are best of friends and talk just about every day. David has had a number of health issues the past three years, some of which have been life threatening. He has had quite a few outpatient surgeries and on one of these occasions, he asked if I would be willing to drive him to and from the hospital since he would be heavily sedated. Of course, I said I would be happy to.

When I take "Phoenix" with me, he generally is in my purse with his head popping out on one end. On the morning I picked David up to take him to the hospital, he was aware I had "Phoenix" with me. The first time I showed my stuffed dog to David, he burst into tears, literally. He was so moved by the likeness, as well as the presence this stuffed dog exudes. So, after we arrived at the hospital and David was checked in, the staff began preparing David for his surgery. The nurse, who would be assisting, introduced herself and informed me of the procedure they would be performing on David that day. Then I pulled "Phoenix" out of my purse and asked her if my (stuffed) dog could be in the room with David. I told her that I knew it may sound strange, but that I believed "Phoenix" would "help" with the surgery. She took one look at the dog and said, "Yes, absolutely!" She got it! So, I released the dog to her care and discretion, and off I went to the waiting room.

After the surgery, I was called into the recovery area where the nurse with whom I had left "Phoenix" met me. She carefully handed my stuffed dog back to me. The words she then spoke did not surprise me at all. She said, "You know, in some way I believe this dog really did help." She went on to explain that the doctor at the beginning of surgery was not so sure how things were going to go because of a delicate issue that was present. I thanked her for her cooperation and care, and we parted company. Meanwhile, David recovered quite nicely and before he knew it, he was stable at home resting quietly.

There have been so many "magical" incidents surrounding the dynamic of this little stuffed dog that probably could be a book in itself. By this time, one really has to ask oneself, "So what is real?"

I once read somewhere that this question was posed to a wise man on his deathbed. When he was asked what was real, his response was, "What is real is that which never changes." "Holy Cow," I thought as I read that, because what could possibly not change?

I was moved beyond words when I realized the answer: "Love without condition."

So, now when people approach me and say, "Oh I thought that was a real dog," I simply smile and say, "It is."

Cassie

9
Subtleties:
From Rescue To Recognition

*"Only when we truly recognize the God within everything, can there be true honor.
When honor is present, there is nothing to rescue."* — Jane Lí

"Let nothing disturb you. Let nothing frighten you. Everything passes away except God."
- Saint Theresa 1515- 1582

In this final chapter, I find myself feeling great humility accompanied by a strong sense of expansion. I believe as a people we are expanding way beyond our old "boxes" of how things "should be" and are beginning to embody what "can be." The old must be let go, in order for the new to emerge. I acknowledge this can appear to be easier said than done. What is the cost to ourselves and those around us by continuing to hang onto that which does not serve us? In our expanded state of consciousness, we are infinite as well as limitless beings. We have convinced ourselves otherwise way too long.

There are really no boundaries to hold us. We have however, held ourselves hostage in a sense, to concepts, rules, and mental structures (which I refer to as "**boxes**") that are nothing more than self-made "prisons." Here's the good news: We also hold the "**key**" to free ourselves.

My wish for this chapter is that it will provide the reader impetus for radical change that will emanate from within. Change that will, in turn, create a shift so amazingly powerful, that it will catapult you into the entire "new" reality, never to look back. I am simply requesting that you, the reader, will consider what I am saying and be open to exploring this expanded perspective. Let the transformation begin!

The subject of animal rescue can be a very delicate subject. It can range anywhere from abusive situations to environmental circumstances where we feel the need to step in and do something to help. *I want to be as clear as possible that I am not saying we should not be assisting in these types of situations. Nor am I saying we should not have certain organizations for these situations when they arise.*

However, when we embody the awareness that "thoughts are things" and realize we have the creative ability to shift our own reality, consider this:

If our thoughts are focused on rescue, we will forever be "rescuing." This does not only fall into the category of animals. The pattern of "rescue" has been so prevalent throughout history in a number of forms, and runs so deep at so many levels; it can seem impervious to our perception.

I believe this pattern of "rescue" has its roots in the desire to be "taken care of." If we will but look around us in our world as we "think" we know it, wanting to be "taken care of" and/or to be rescued, is at epidemic proportions. In and of itself there is nothing wrong with "taking care." Where it gets jaded is, so often we give our power away to those whom we "think" have a better idea or can do something for us that we "think" we cannot do for ourselves. This has been the underpinnings of the microcosm to the macrocosm for centuries. We have all played into the "rescue me" mentality and/or program to the proportion that we keep recreating this dynamic moment by moment. When we embody that mentality of wanting to be rescued ourselves, we then attempt to find things that need to be rescued, and so it goes. Also, when we see things that appear ill, weak, or helpless, the tendency is to want to fix or rescue.

Remember, thoughts are things and energy follows thought. Along with this, we hold within ourselves the ability to be well, when we are "ill." We are designed that way. If we do not heal, there is usually a reason which has nothing to do with anything outside of ourselves. To quote Albert Einstein, "You cannot solve a problem with the same mind that created it." This may involve scripting a new story line for ourselves if the one we've been living currently does not portray honor with ourselves. The "perceived" problems arise when we allow ourselves to be "stuck" in our story within a limited identity, and forget that our choices and options are limitless.

Guess what? This also includes our friends in fur coats. This is where "God in fur" comes into play in a most significant and profound way. If we watch very carefully with "x-ray" vision, it's as if the entire reason for these creatures being here is to remind us that it is always "playtime." We all, myself included, have taken our lives much too seriously. Seriousness creates "density" and interrupts the flow of joy that so much wants to show up. I believe at a primordial level, we know this, and it is exactly the reason so many of us choose to surround ourselves with "God" donning a fur coat.

In order for us to actually see ourselves from the outside of what we are really up to here on planet Earth, we as a "collective consciousness" must "let go" of our old stories in order to realize a shift into a higher gear or frequency. This, in turn, will enable us to recognize who we are and move way beyond any need to be "rescued" or to be a "rescuer."

For example, one gorgeous afternoon in downtown Kirkland, I was working outdoors. I was trimming a hedge at one of my landscaping accounts. I love being outdoors working because in this particular area of Kirkland there are no end of folks out walking their dogs. Usually within about an hour or two, I am presented with opportunities to interact with "God" on a leash … Pure Fun! So on this particular day, a man came up the road walking two dogs. I put down my tools, approached this gentleman and asked if I could pet his dogs. One dog was quite large and the other quite small. I began to pet and interact with the smaller dog first. I no sooner did this when the man spoke up and said, "Oh, she is my rescue," I found his verbiage a bit odd, but I had no response, I just continued interacting with the dogs. I knew this man felt compelled to tell me his rescue story of this dog. It came across and felt like the dog somehow was his "project," and the man was admiring his "handiwork." It also felt as though this man had told this story many times.

You see, this is what it is to be stuck in a story. In this man's mind, the dog will always be a dog he rescued, which is extremely limiting for him and the dog. Whenever we create the illusion of being stuck in a story, especially if it is not a fun and uplifting one, we fail to see that there can be a myriad of possible outcomes, *and that we can choose any one we like*. When we are busy rescuing, we are not focused on the essence of what we think we are rescuing. What's more, we *cannot "see" because the focus is on helplessness and victimhood.*

In contrast, if we do recognize the essence, we will also recognize what the situation may be bringing to us and how it is an "out-picturing" or a mirror for us to see aspects of ourselves more clearly. If we look behind the façade of any "rescue" attempts, there is pure gold for us, through the trappings disguised in fur.

Another aspect I want to cover briefly is that of "judgment." This one thing will keep us stuck for what will feel like eternity. Judgment can be so very subtle. Most of what we "think" we see in the first place are nothing but perceptions that originate from our own "boxes" or "filters" that we hold as "truth," and at times we will fight to the death defending these perceptions when we have our identity or judgment attached with it. If this sounds like struggle, it is. This is not a fun way to live, nor is it an environment for thriving.

Judgment can become a very addictive pattern because usually before we know it, we have bought into a drama of what we have judged, as worthy of our attention. Then we attempt to solicit others to join us in our drama to perpetuate it. This is so prevalent when it comes to animal rescue. It is impossible to recognize or feel the essence of anything when we are in judgment.

The linear mind wants to judge because most times it gets a "charge" from being a rescuer and feeling "right." Consequently, others must be judged as "wrong" by the mind to preserve our identity as being "right." It takes practice and paying attention to begin to dismantle the energetic pattern of judgment. Choosing to observe what we are thinking about is a good starting point. Shedding a tiny bit of light (by our observing what we are thinking) has the potential to diffuse a whole lot of unwanted things.

The other aspect of this dismantling of judgment patterns is that of love without condition. Whenever we "let go" of energetic or emotional baggage from judgment, our hearts become more open because we are literally creating space for more love to be resident within. So, we could say the "dismantling" creates the space for the "energy" to rearrange itself in a new and higher frequency. This will attract more of the "adamantine particles" and increase our ability to love without condition. More love attracts more love, and so it goes. So really, what does this have to do with God in fur? Everything.

It appears that the energy on our beautiful planet we call Earth is speeding up. I believe this because things are now accelerating in this fast moving stream of energy. You can find this energetic and earthly "acceleration" discussed through multiple internet resources when you search, "the Precession of the Equinox" online. This accelerated energy affects our dogs' and other pets' well being as they share the burden of any resistance to these changes *by us*. Our dogs and animals in general, are not as easily able or willing, to shoulder or carry our issues in their bodies any longer; nor should they. They deserve to be loved without condition, and live in environments where they are able to thrive. We have been, and are currently seeing the effects in our animals that are exposed to these stressful conditions.

When God Wears Fur

I read somewhere just recently that hummingbirds will avoid places where they sense harshness. This is not surprising. As an example, when my former husband David and I were together, a good portion of the time unrest and disharmony was in our home. I now know how that environment greatly contributed to our beloved Phoenix and his ongoing illnesses. I even recall times where I would observe Phoenix looking for a way out of the house if voices were raised in anger … Now, there's a clue.

To this point, our pets have been willing to assist us in seeing ourselves. However, if we refuse to shift by making the necessary "adjustments" in our consciousness they will find a way to take their leave. This may play out as an illness, running away, or in extreme cases, being hit by a car. This may sound harsh but I have heard quite a few stories to validate what I am saying. It is, however, important to remember here that because everything is made up of energy, nothing ever "dies." This is especially helpful to keep in mind when we hear stories or see atrocities being done to animals at the hands of humans.

Whether we are a concerned private citizen or part of an animal rights organization educating and providing humane treatment to animals, shifting a reality of mistreatment of all animals is not *completely changed* by that alone. All any of us have is this current moment where we can choose to be present in love no matter what. May we let go of the past, and judgment of ourselves, and others, regarding these situations.

Throughout history there have been voices of those crying in the wilderness telling us that there is a better or higher way for all of us to live. Now these voices are reaching "critical mass." An awakening is occurring that cannot be stopped. If we do not yet "see" it, we are all feeling it. One of my very favorite quotes is that of the late Mahatma Gandhi who said, "We must be the change we want to see in the world."

If change is not being generated from within our own self (by letting go of judgment of ourselves and others with love), we then can become a slave to "fixing" and "rescuing" to which there is no end. We will chain ourselves to "good causes" and use massive amounts of energy doing so. When we begin to live our lives from a perception that **we are not separate from our source of love**, knowing from within that "all is well," we will begin to see a reality play out where that is indeed experienced. We will also begin to see more wellness, more joy, more acceptance, and more of what we would label as "miraculous." Our friends in fur will then also feel these benefits.

Now is the time for us to shift into a reality where "all things are possible" in any given moment. Love without condition will open the door to that reality. Recognizing ourselves for the limitless beings that we are, we will begin to see the same in all creations. We will make the shift from "surviving" to "thriving." Life is supposed to be a fun, joyous experience of health, abundance, and "well-being" for all. Phoenix was and is a stellar example of these very things. His playful loving presence never failed to "show up" for the party.

My closing wish is that everyone who has journeyed with me throughout these pages will begin to live in a reality where every day is a day of magic and miracles. Also, that each day will grow sweeter and sweeter; that in every breath, we will breathe in abundance and health, and that every furry creature we meet, we will recognize as "God in fur."

Namaste,

Jane Lí

In Tribute to My Beloved Phoenix, "God" Disguised as a Dog:

When God Wears Fur

When God wears fur, people stop and stare,
when God wears fur, it happens everywhere.

The wagging of tails, the eyes filled with love,
none is greater than this, for it arrives "from above."

All shapes and sizes, adorning our coats with style,
never a paw turning back, for all of life is worthwhile.

We'll play catch the day long, we each have our own song.

We're no different than you, as you're beginning to see;
We even like the same foods; there's no "you" and no "me."

For we are all just reflections, 'cause this life is a mirror,
and we have come to show you: just why you are here.

We love our disguises, though you may not be aware;
So be honorable in how you treat us,
with only the best of care.

For God has many faces,
Too many to name, and that is for sure.

But that feeling of love unconditional,
Unmistakable, unlike any other,

Is when God wears fur.

Jane Li

Tuck

"Golden Milkbones" for Expansion and Transformation

Books I Highly Recommend:

- *The Field*, by Lynn McTaggert ... A scientific exploration how physics and spiritual realities are joined showing evidence how we are "not separate', but all connected. This book also educates the reader on scientific existence of "Morphic fields."

- *The Power of Now* by Eckhart Tolle ... The present of presence in the magical "now" moment: a practical guide.

- *Love Without End*, by Glenda Green ...*Remarkable expansion of love without condition.*

- *Matrix Energetics*, by Dr. Richard Bartlett, DC, ND ...When things are not labeled as a "problem," all things are possible.

- *Feng Shui For Horses*, by Jane Lí Fox ... How to really "listen" to and be "one" with your pet.

- *The Pocketbook of Transformation and Transcendence*, by Karen Cornell, Marlene Putnam, and Jane Lí Fox ... Fun, practical explanations of transforming realities.

Wonderful Movies for Exiting the "Box":

- *Seabiscuit* ... For seeing the "impossible" be possible.

- *Mr. Magorium's Wonder Emporium* ... Life is joyous as well as magical, as we awaken to who we are.

- *The Last Mimzy* ... Depicts the infinite beings that we are.

- *Forrest Gump* ... A perfect example of what life can be like when we live in non-resistance.

- *Yes Man* ... Learning to say "yes" to life.

Monty

Glossary

Adamantine Particles: "Particles containing a continuous flow of high frequency potential which manifest into discrete forms and arrangements under the command of Love." A full discussion and definition is contained in all of Chapter 5 of *Love Without End*, by Glenda Green (beginning on page 101)

Morphic Fields: "As recognized in physics, fields are non-material regions of influence, of patterns of information and 'action at a distance'. Through them objects not in physical contact may still affect each other." — Page 12 of Matrix Energetics Seminars 1 & 2 Syllabus by Dr. Richard Bartlett, DC, ND, author of *Matrix Energetics*.

Parallel Universes: "Quantum science suggests the existence of many possible futures for each moment of our lives. Each future lies in a state of rest until it is awakened by choices made in the present." — Gregg Braden, Scientist and visionary scholar bridging science and spirituality.

Channeling: "The bringing forth of profound knowledge and information from unseen sources of intelligence" — Jane Lí Fox

Linear Mind: "This is what I call the 'Box': a mind that is based completely on what is seen or perceived only by the naked human eye. It is one-dimensional and cannot perceive the unseen world simply because there is no 'equation' for it to be accepted in this type of 'Box' mind set." — Jane Lí Fox

Coco

About The Author

Jane Lí Fox lives in western Washington. She has been beautifying and clearing people's homes for over 30 years. Her keen eye, along with her love of nature and animals, has enabled her to create a niche for herself by incorporating her intuitive expertise to assist her clients and their animals with moving through life with more ease. She has loved many clients, many dear friends, and family members, who readily agree that Jane Lí co-creates a space of well-being and love around all people, animals, and plants she interacts with on a daily basis.

Jane Lí has published many prose and poetry works besides *When God Wears Fur*. Most recently, she authored *Feng Shui For Horses*. She shares how Feng Shui's energetic "flow" principles relates in the care of horses, and how to truly "listen" and be "one" with your horse with Quantum Physics awareness. *In Request of Honor*, a very moving article about the passing of her horse, Prince, she reflects on the impact of how he and other horses have loyally and valiantly served humankind on many levels. Inspired again by Prince, she is currently working on a trilogy about a little girl and her magical horse.

Also, Jane Lí Fox has co-authored and published *The Pocketbook of Prosperity, Peace and Personal Power, The Pocketbook of Relationships, and The Pocketbook of Transformation and Transcendence*, with Karen Cornell and Marlene Putnam.

I have known Jane Lí and her family for over twenty years, and watched her consistent loving heart expand. I have witnessed, or heard first hand, many synchronicities or miracles that came to pass at her command or loving influence. She is always so excited and thankful at every single one, no matter how large or small, and never takes anything for granted. I, and so many others touched by her love, experience the reality that it is the "Love unconditional," which sparks miracles in our daily lives, if we but include it in our awareness.

The last few years in particular, I would try to save all of Jane Lí's voice-mailed accounts of the latest daily miracles and synchronicities, until my saved log would become too full, repeatedly. Assisting her by typing and editing "When God Wears Fur" was a surreal experience, as I knew her dog Phoenix personally. During that time, I had many phone conversations with Jane Lí as well as phone messages about the "moment-by-moment" accounts of what transpired during his last health challenges and final transition process. There is so much more I witnessed of Jane Lí's experiences after Phoenix's passing ... but you will have to read the book to find out yourself!

— *Bev McCaw, Assisting Editor and longtime friend*

More Furry Friends for the Limelight

Spanky Li

Gruffud

Spencer

Wally

Gruffud

Tuck

Cassie

Gruffud

Tuck

Spencer

In Memoriam

Sasha departed this world in Fall 2010. We love you, Sasha.

www.ingramcontent.com/pod-product-compliance
Lightning Source LLC
LaVergne TN
LVHW090047090426
835511LV00031B/462